Towns and Villages OF ENGLAND

HIGHWORTH

GRAHAM TANNER

ALAN SUTTON

First published in the United Kingdom in 1993 by
Alan Sutton Publishing Ltd · Phoenix Mill · Far Thrupp · Stroud
Gloucestershire

First published in the United States of America in 1993 by
Alan Sutton Publishing Inc. · 83 Washington Street · Dover
NH 03820

British Library Cataloguing in Publication Data

Tanner, Graham
  Towns and Villages of England: Highworth
  I. Title
  942.31

  ISBN 0-7509-0551-4

Library of Congress Cataloging in Publication Data applied for

Typeset in Bembo 11/13pt.
Typesetting and origination by
Alan Sutton Publishing Limited.
Printed in Great Britain by
Hartnolls Ltd, Bodmin, Cornwall.

Contents

Detail from Taylor & Blome's map of Wiltshire (*c.* 1715) showing Highworth's position and significance relative to other settlements

CHAPTER ONE

Highworth: Its Situation, Geology and Early History

In the north-east corner of Wiltshire, close to the convergence of Gloucestershire, Oxfordshire, Wiltshire and pre-1974 Berkshire, some six miles north of Swindon is Highworth, pleasantly situated on a hill which commands extensive views over the surrounding green down country. To the east stretches the Vale of White Horse, which takes its name from the eponymous white horse cut high up on the downs' escarpment above Uffington, which has overlooked the Vale for countless ages, and which is watered by the upper reaches of the River Thames. To the south rise the Marlborough and Berkshire Downs; while to the north-westward the East Cotswolds of Gloucestershire and Oxon provide the horizon.

View to the south of the Berkshire Downs

Approaching Highworth one is immediately aware of the hill upon which it stands; the very name of the town being ample evidence of the position it occupies, standing above the Upper Thames valley, some 133 metres above mean sea level. Since the earliest times the human settlement upon the hill top and its slopes has been inextricably linked with the geology of the area, and the topographical position. The rock upon which Highworth stands was laid down in the Jurassic period some 150 million years ago, producing the Coral Rag, which becomes the dominant outcrop, and would appear to indicate that the sea over Wiltshire at this period was considerably warmer than it is today, so enabling the fossil corals so frequently encountered in the surrounding arable fields to flourish.

This Corallian outcrop which runs from the airfield at RAF Lyneham via Swindon widens to form an escarpment including Blunsdon, Hannington and Highworth hills which overlooks the valley of the Upper Thames, and of its tributary, the Cole, which forms the north-eastern boundary of the County of Wiltshire. This easily accessible building material was quarried by early settlers in Highworth for the random stone dwellings of the town. Until relatively recently the area around Highworth was dotted with small quarries where outcrops of coral rag had been excavated as a building material. Intensive agricultural practice has however led to most of these quarries being filled and brought into production; to my knowledge only one such quarry remains, that being adjacent to the south-west corner of the golf course in Botany Fields, where the contours of the land would make filling impracticable. The sites of the other quarries are clearly indicated on the 1926 Edition of the 6 inch Ordnance Survey maps of the area, and they can be identified at times of ploughing by the difference in soil, and occasionally by the discovery of bottles etc included in the in-fill.

At Red Down the name derives from the iron rich red loam with its characteristic reddish brown colour which overlays the Oxford Clay, and marks the spring line which surrounds Highworth Hill, and which must have been an important factor in the settlement of the area. Outcrops of the yellow 'Highworth Grit' sand are to be found in the slopes leading to the hill top, these, interestingly, providing in Botany Fields and at the Butts (above the old railway line) the sites of extensive rabbit warrens, apparently the Highworth Grit being a geological stratum preferred by rabbits! A further extensive outcrop of Highworth Grit was to be found in the quarry in Station Road adjacent to the railway station, which as well as being worked for building material provided a natural habitat for the sand martin, and in the days of birds egg collecting an interesting diversion for the youth of the town when able to avoid the attentions of 'Happy' Painter, the farmer who owned Home Farm (opposite St Michael's parish church) in whose fields the quarry was situated.

Although Highworth is part of that area of north-east Wiltshire described by H.S. Tallamy as 'always just slightly off the map of history, until the Railway Age . . .', recent evidence suggests that there is a great deal more to the history of Highworth than had previously been considered.

Work in the 1970s by the Highworth Historical Society and the Swindon Archaeology Society built upon previous finds from the 1930s, and established the existence of Iron Age and later Roman settlements in the Hampton Hill area of the town. Excavation revealed the remains of an Iron Age settlement in the northern extension of the cemetery in Cricklade Road, together with a series of Iron Age pits containing examples of 'worked' flints.

During development of the Haresfield Estate on the north-eastern side of the town further finds of flint tools were made, the scale of the finds being such as to suggest that an occupation site existed near to The Willows and Partridge Place. M.J. Stone suggests that the sites discovered around Highworth were likely to be those of temporary camps, which were on well drained sand or silt and close to the line of springs which surround the town, and possessed the advantage of elevation on Hampton Hill and the slopes of Highworth Hill; they date from the later Mesolithic period some 6000 to 4000 BC.

With the Roman Ermine Street (joining Corinium (Cirencester) to Silchester) some three miles south of Highworth, the discovery of a Roman villa at Stanton Fitzwarren and a further villa at Hannington Wick, it is unsurprising that evidence of Roman settlement should be found at Highworth. The development of the Wrde Hill and Roman Way housing estate in the 1960s provided considerable evidence that this area was well populated during the Roman period, with finds including pottery, coins, tiles, jewellery and a burial area all dating from the second to fourth centuries AD.

Further finds during the development of the Haresfield estate clearly indicate the existence of a Romano-British settlement in the area of Priory Green, and of several substantial villa-farms and smaller agricultural settlements in the surrounding countryside. Clear evidence that there had been an appreciable degree of Roman influence on those who lived on and around Highworth Hill during the period of the first to fourth centuries AD.

The next stage in the historical development of the town is provided not by Highworth itself, but rather those parts known as Eastrop and Westrop. 'Thorp' or 'trop' is Danish in origin, meaning 'enclosed ground' as in Westrop and Eastrop, and with the Danes contending with the Saxon settlers in the neighbourhood of Chippenham as early as AD 866 and overrunning North Wiltshire in AD 995 it is fair to suggest that these settlements existed before Highworth; and that they were east and west of each other, and not of Highworth, which demonstrably they are not. In all probability the settlements of Eastrop and Westrop, appreciably earlier than Highworth, would have been dependent upon the water supply, both Eastrop and Westrop being upon the spring line encircling Highworth Hill, while the task of sinking wells into the rock of the plateau was beyond the contemporary technology.

Further circumstantial evidence is provided by the presence in the locality of many wych-elders, or Danes Blood, the hedge shrub introduced by the Danes.

The first extant mention of Highworth itself is in the Domesday Book, compiled on the orders of William the Conqueror and completed in AD 1086, and which is the main authority for these times. The entry pertaining to Highworth, but given under Wrde (Worth) – probably Saxon and denoting a farmstead or an enclosed place, the epithet 'high' not being added until the thirteenth century, and being self evident – read 'From early days Radulphus, a priest, holds the church of Wrde, and three hides belong to it which are not assessed. Two ploughlands: the priest occupies these with six borders and ten acres of meadow. It is worth 100 shillings.'

Despite being one of the only two churches recorded in the area – the other was at Cricklade – Highworth was of little significance at the time of the Domesday Survey.

As Lawton suggests 'Archaeological and documentary evidence suggests that Highworth was a relatively late settlement despite the fact that Highworth hill has seen almost continuous occupation for about 4000 years.' As suggested earlier the early settlements are those at Eastrop and Westrop along with Hampton, Sevenhampton and Inglesham.

Sevenhampton is also mentioned in the Domesday Book as part of the possession of William, Earl of Ewe or Ow, whose descendants retained it until the reign of Henry III. It was forfeited to the Crown and given to Prince Edward, afterwards Edward I, and was later to become the property of the Warneford family.

Haslam, discussing the development of Highworth in this period, suggests that 'The description of Highworth in Domesday is that of a small village only; no burgesses are mentioned. The Manor and Hundred of Highworth are supposed to have been established by charter of Edward I. Fuller documentary work must be undertaken on Highworth before anything more detailed about its history in the medieval period can be said. Highworth is another example of a thirteenth-century planted town, with market-place, main street and a church behind, laid out in a regular pattern. The property boundaries of the original burgage plots are still clearly fossilized in the modern property boundaries. The tythe barn as well as some fishponds also existed in the medieval period.'

Such fishponds when found in groups of two or three in tiers, placed thus for purposes of purifying, are generally evidence of a monastery in the neighbourhood. However, despite the fishponds there is no evidence to support the existence of a monastery in Highworth.

Evidence from the poll tax returns of the later medieval period indicate a continuing growth for Highworth, so that it ranked alongside Purton, Cricklade and Ashton Keynes as being one of the most important places in the area.

Hopkins claims that 'Highworth used, in the earliest days, to return a member of Parliament. A writ was addressed to the bailiffs in the 26th of Edward I, to which no return was made.' Elective franchise was never afterwards exercised, although writs continued to be sent to the bailiffs until the 24th of Edward IV. After that all rights of franchise were ceded to the Borough of Lechlade.

The Manor and ancient Hundred of Highworth are supposed to have been established by charter of Edward I (cf. Haslam) and even up to the beginning of the nineteenth century a court of pleas or court of barons was still being held for this Manor and Hundred, in which debts under the sum of 40 shillings were recoverable.

Aerial photography of the Highworth area by a Major Allen in the early 1930s discovered evidence of a number of circular earthworks in the vicinity

Earthworks at Common Farm

of the town. Initially these were thought to be of Roman origin, but recent examination has placed them in the twelfth to thirteenth centuries. There is a total of forty-eight such enclosures in the area, with banks outside the ditch and single entrances. Some are circular, and may have been cattle pounds; some are square with rounded corners, and may have enclosed manorial buildings. Rings of this type have not been identified elsewhere, and have as a result been known as the Highworth type.

The ensuing years saw an increase in the population of Highworth which naturally created a demand for more houses. The south side of the High Street contains buildings from the fifteenth and sixteenth centuries, including the Manor House, an example of a fifteenth-century hall house, while a plank-and-muntin partition alongside a cross-passage dates the King & Queen Inn as being of a similar date. The houses on the north side of the High Street date from between 1600 and 1630. Hence by the time of the Civil War the town had become a place of some importance.

With the advent of the Civil War the natural position of St Michael's church brought some trouble upon itself, the church tower providing an excellent look-out over the Thames Valley and a lofty firing platform. A situation which was to be replicated almost three centuries later when the local Home Guard used the tower for similar reasons in the expected but never realized 'Operation Sealion'!

The Manor House in the High Street

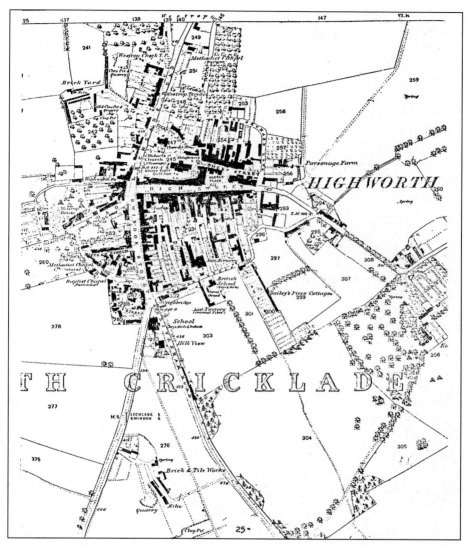

Large scale map of Highworth, clearly showing the medieval layout of the town

The church had been fortified in late 1644, and on 27 June 1645 Major Hen of the Royal Garrison was holding it for the King, but was summoned to surrender by the Parliamentary forces under Fairfax on their way to Taunton after the Battle of Naseby. When Major Hen refused to yield, the Parliamentary forces planted their ordnance and prepared to storm the church. Despite Major Hen taking down his colours and yielding, it appears

Tower of St Michael's church dominating
the town and countryside

that at least one round of ball was fired by the Parliamentary ordnance, as is
evidenced by the damage on the west door of the church, and the ball
preserved as a relic within the church.

Local folklore has held that the ball was fired from a field west of the
church at Hampton commonly referred to as 'the humpty-dumps'; and that
the irregularities of the surface of this field were as a result of the dead from
the ensuing battle being buried there. It appears extremely doubtful that an
ordnance piece of this time could project a ball over this range, or with this
degree of accuracy. A more likely explanation is that the ball was fired from
Home Farm opposite the church, as recent excavations in the area have
produced evidence of a defensive ditch some six feet wide, along with a 'V'
shaped earth bank from which defensive fire could be given.

In the event the followers of Fairfax found good booty in the church
taking seventy prisoners and eighty arms, the whole affair being over in some
three hours.

Hopkins reports that 'Many skeletons have been dug up at the west end of
the church, and in the surrounding country some of the remains of those
killed in the fight, and many possibly of those who died from the Plague in
1666.'

Aubrey, the seventeenth-century antiquarian, describes the situation as being that 'At Highworth was the greatest market, on Wednesday, for fatt cattle in our county, which was furnished by the rich vale; and the Oxford butchers furnished themselves here. In the late civill warres it being made a garrison for the King, the grasiers, to avoid the rudeness of the souldiers, quitted that market, and went to Swindon four miles distant, where the market on Munday continues still, which before was a petty, inconsiderable one. Also, the plague was at Highworth before the late Warres, which was very prejudiciall to the market there; by reason whereof all the countrey sent their cattle to Swindown market, as they did before to Highworth.'

Growth during the eighteenth century was slow, since Highworth was a market town with agriculture being the source of economic wealth and of employment. During the greater part of this century farming still utilized the two-fold rotation, with a permanent common – the present day Common Farm – being clear evidence of this, while many unimproved pasture fields in the neighbourhood bear evidence of the ridge and furrow of the two-field system. Enclosure of the land around Highworth finally took place in 1778–9.

The change from the two-fold system, where each farmer had strips of land scattered over the two fields with the right to pasture animals on the

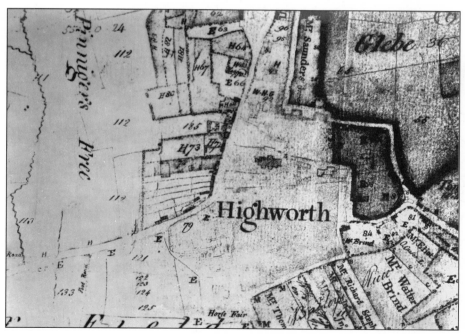

Enclosure map of Highworth

9

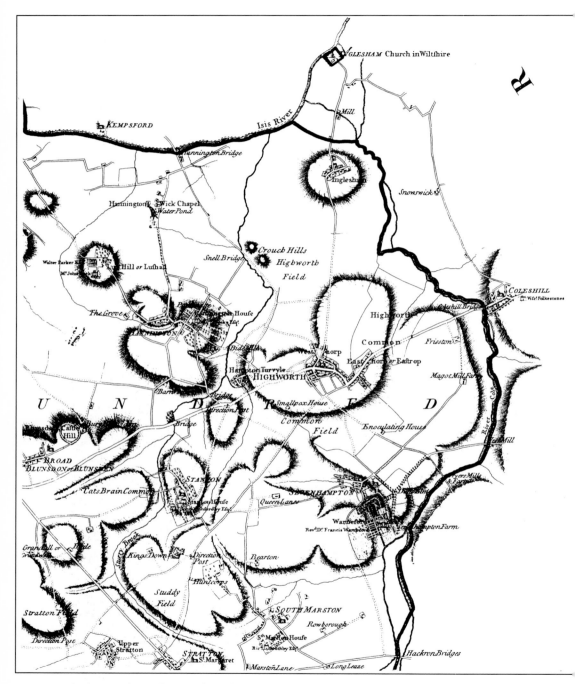

Andrews and Dury's map of Wiltshire, 1773

common, to enclosed farming usually brought changes in the style of farming from a style which was predominantly arable to one more involved with animal husbandry. Arable farming had at this time been heavily labour intensive, whereas dairy or sheep farming required far less labour. As a result a large number of farm labourers and small farmers lost their means of livelihood. Those requiring further coverage of the enclosure of Highworth are referred to Lawton, *Enclosure 1778–1783*.

The eighteenth century in Highworth ended on a particularly low note with, in 1790, a disastrous outbreak of smallpox. To bring the outbreak under control the entire population of the town had to be inoculated. Such inoculations required the isolation of those involved until they ceased to be a carrier of the disease. To assure this Highworth had two such houses, the Inoculating House alongside the Shrivenham road, near 'Hangman's Elms', and the Smallpox House in Botany Fields immediately behind the ninth tee on the Thamesdown Golf Course (see Andrews & Dury's map of 1773).

However, the close of the eighteenth century in Highworth saw a distinct improvement with the national growth of property and population reflected in the town.

Examples of typical Highworth Goss Ware

CHAPTER TWO

1800 to 1939

In common with the rest of England, Highworth's population continued to grow during the early years of the nineteenth century, the first census, that of 1801, returning a population of some 2,200. In part this increase in population was as a result of Britain's increasing wealth and prosperity, which brought in its train a powerful feeling of national confidence. Parallel to these economic improvements were those related to the control of epidemic disease and illness. In this connection Cassey's Directory of 1861 shows two 'surgeons' and one chemist in Highworth, the latter doubling as a brewer! Quack doctors abounded, claiming to cure every conceivable complaint in man or beast, as did apothecaries who travelled to the markets and fairs peddling their own and later proprietary remedies whose efficacy was guaranteed. However many still preferred the use of familiar herbal remedies obtained either from the local 'wise' woman, or made by themselves.

By the 1841 census Highworth's population had reached its nineteenth-century maximum of some 4,000, a figure which was not to be reached again until the mid-twentieth century, the decline continuing from the 1840s until the early 1920s when the population was some 2,000. In part the emigration from Highworth during the 1840s was as a result of the siting of the Great Western Railway works at Swindon. Brunel had set about researching two alternative approaches for the GWR west of Reading, one through Newbury, Savernake Forest, Pewsey Vale to Bath and Bristol; the other going through the Thames Valley and north of the Marlborough Downs with gradients virtually nil for many miles. The refusal of the Marquis of Ailesbury to countenance the Great Western Railway passing through Savernake Forest meant that Highworth's chances of remaining the dominant market town on the hill, with Swindon's address continuing to be near Highworth, ended. Brunel and Gooch's picnic on the future site of the Great Western works finally ensured that Highworth remained firmly under the influence of Swindon. Hence the need for those who sought employment in the GWR works to emigrate to Swindon, a need which remained paramount until a reliable means of transport existed.

A reliable and relatively speedy means of transport to Swindon became a reality in 1883 when the Swindon to Highworth branch railway line was opened for public use. This together with the opening in the early 1870s of the Oriental Fibre Mat & Matting Company in Brewery Street provided jobs, and transport to jobs for those living in the town, and hence halted the decline in the population of Highworth.

Despite the number of Highworthians working in the Great Western Railway works, Highworth remained predominantly an agricultural town, and the decline in the population paralleled that occurring in agriculture nationally, reflecting at least in part the increasing mechanization of farming.

From the 1880s, with the coming of the railway to the town and the opening of the mat factory, life settled into the relatively quiet pattern of a small market town, broken only by such national celebrations as Queen Victoria's Diamond Jubilee in 1897, and the coronation of King Edward VII in 1902, when in common with the rest of the realm Highworth was 'en fete', with the town decorated overall and in great celebration. With the celebration of the opening of the twentieth century, Highworth enjoyed a period of calm, but little development, and attempted to improve the level of trade through the new branch railway line to Swindon and through the cattle market which was held on the last Wednesday of each month (except for the December market which was held on the first Wednesday after the eighth of the month).

However in September 1909 Highworth's years of calm were for a period shattered by a portent of the happenings to come in five years' time. In August of that year General Sir John French, the Inspector General to the Army and responsible as such for military training, had selected the area around Faringdon and Highworth for the year's army manoeuvres.

These manoeuvres began on Monday 20 September and lasted for three days. The scenario was that the 'Red' and 'Blue' forces faced each other across a frontier defined by the River Thames from Reading in the east to Cricklade in the west, and then by the Thames and Severn and Stroudwater Canals to the River Severn. ('Red' territory was to the north of this frontier, with its capital at Northampton, and 'Blue' territory to the south with Salisbury as its capital.)

The 'Blue' forces were initially at Malmesbury, Wootton Bassett and Swindon, while those of the opposing 'Red' forces were based at Burford, Witney, Woodstock and Cheltenham. By nightfall on the Monday the 'Red' forces had laid siege to Faringdon, while General Sir Arthur Paget brought in troops for its defence.

The Queen's Regiment of the 'Blue' forces was drawn into the defence of Faringdon from their base at Malmesbury, and their route brought them to Highworth.

Photographs show the Queen's resting in Highworth before their march to Faringdon, and also show a horse-drawn pontoon in the High Street. Other

The Queen's Regiment resting in the High Street

photographs show the motor cars of various foreign attachés parked in the Market Square *en route* to observe the battle for Faringdon.

The *Evening Advertiser* reported that 'At Highworth, people turned out in great numbers to watch the progress of columns through the town. At the corner of Market Street (High Street) groups of officers and men had been coming and going all the morning while motor-cars, in greater numbers perhaps than ever seen before in Highworth, were passing and re-passing, carrying officers, foreign attachés and others to the front.'

Local folklore insists that these manoeuvres were also watched by Kaiser Wilhelm of Germany, but this is certainly a case of mistaken identity, further embroidered by the happenings in five years' time. None the less many Highworth worthies of the period are prepared to testify to having seen 'Kaiser Bill' at Highworth!

As the 'Blue' army retreated from Faringdon with the 3rd Division retreating towards Shrivenham, and the 5th Division seeking to re-group around Coleshill, the 'Red' 2nd Division chose to attack at Shrivenham, while their 1st Division was counter-attacked from the west (i.e. from the Highworth direction) by the Blues. The ensuing battle covered an arc of some eight miles from the south-west of Faringdon, through Coleshill to Shrivenham.

The encounter was described as 'a brilliant spectacle lasting for many hours but without any result being achieved. Indeed Mr Asquith and Mr Haldane waited in vain on Badbury Hill for an assault on their position and would have missed the final infantry battle altogether had they not motored to an adjacent hill.'

By 5 o'clock on the Wednesday afternoon the manoeuvres had ended, with the East Yorkshires having made a forced march from Highworth in the heat of a late summer day.

However, in the short space of five years, troops who had fought their 'war games' over the countryside surrounding, together with many young men from the town, were involved in all the horrors which were to be part of the 'war to end wars' – The Great War of 1914–18 – in which some thirty-nine Highworthians laid down their lives in the service of King and Country.

One of these young men, Flight Sub-Lieutenant Reginald Warneford RN of Warneford Place, Sevenhampton, entered the annals of history, not only that of Highworth, but also of the Royal Naval Air Service and of aerial warfare in general.

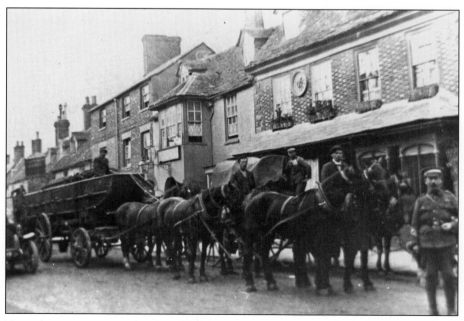

Horse-drawn pontoons in the High Street

By the spring of 1915 the menace of the German Zeppelins was clearly apparent, and on 31 May the Zeppelin LZ 38 carried out the first air raid on London, having previously attacked Margate and Dover in the early hours of 17 May.

In the early hours of 7 June Flt. Sub. Lt. Warneford took off in his Morane-Saulnier Parasol monoplane from the Belgian aerodrome at Furnes, with the intention of attacking any Zeppelins sighted, whether in flight or in their sheds. A few miles south of Bruges, Warneford sighted the Zeppelin LZ 37, and although only armed with light bombs climbed to attack the Zeppelin.

By 2.15 a.m. the Morane had climbed to 11,000 ft, and as dawn was breaking he was in position above his target. Switching off his engine, he came sweeping round towards the stern of the Zeppelin, calculating the right moment to release his bombs. One hundred and fifty feet above his target Warneford released the first of his bombs, followed by two others. The result was a tremendous explosion which almost tore LZ 37 in two, and immediately engulfed it in flames. Warneford's Morane was caught up in the explosion, at times flying upside down, before regaining control. On regaining control Warneford saw that there was no petrol in his tank, and was forced to glide down to the ground in the early dawn, realizing that he was landing behind the German lines.

Flt. Sub. Lt. Reginald Warneford VC, with his Morane-Saulnier Parasol plane

Reginald Warneford's exploit as seen at home

Spurred on by the unpleasant thought of being taken prisoner he set to work to effect a repair, which he did in fifteen minutes, repairing and reconnecting the offending feed pipe.

Just as he had finished, a squadron of German cavalry came into the area, but Warneford succeeded in taking off, despite being pursued by the cavalry firing their carbines at his departing aeroplane.

With insufficient petrol to reach his base in Furnes, Warneford was forced to land in a French sector of the line when his petrol tank was finally empty. Eventually Warneford convinced the French of his credentials and was re-fuelled, arriving back at St Pol at 10.30 a.m.

Since the news of Warneford's downing of LZ 37 had reached Whitehall the Government realized that this exploit was the very thing needed to boost the morale of a population, who had been led to believe that the war would be over by Christmas 1914. The war showing no signs of ending, rather dragging on into its second year, the population were showing signs of natural depression.

Warneford's name and photograph together with the story of the fate of the Zeppelin was blazoned across the front pages of every newspaper, and provided a ray of brightness among the gloom of the news from the front.

For his exploits Reginald Warneford was awarded the country's highest award for valour, the Victoria Cross, by His Majesty King George V, and the Cross of the Legion of Honour by the President of France.

Sadly on Thursday 17 June 1915 Reginald Warneford lost his life when the Henry Farman F27 biplane he was flying over Paris crashed when approaching to land. He was buried with full naval honours in Brompton Cemetery, a memorial plaque to his exploits being placed in the Warneford Chapel of the parish church of St Michael, and some forty years later was further honoured by the naming of the local secondary school after Highworth's first war hero.

For the families of other Highworthians they too were heroes of the same statue as Reginald Warneford, laying down their lives for King and Country.

Apart from the dread of awaiting an Admiralty or War Office telegram announcing the loss of a loved one or, from 25 February 1918, the problem of the rationing of meat and butter in southern England and, from 14 July, the full rationing of foodstuffs to cope with the country's food shortage, which resulted in an appeal by the Prime Minister to assist with the harvest, life continued in a routine way.

Highworth's local war effort was directed to the provision of classes in nursing and first aid, contributions to the Mayor of Swindon's Local War Fund and support for the Belgian refugees who were billeted in the area.

Memorial plaque to Reginald Warneford in the Warneford Chapel of the parish church

The tythe barn, stone from which was used for the foundations of the war memorial

The Armistice in November 1918 signalled an eventual return to normality, the only permanent reminder of the 'war to end wars' being the erection in 1920 of the cenotaph at the west end of the churchyard to commemorate the 'glorious dead' of the war. In this connection it is interesting to note that stone from the old tythe barn opposite Parsonage Farm was used for the foundations of the cenotaph. The other somewhat less permanent reminders (lasting however until the construction of the MAP bungalows in 1940) were the German railway coaches, which were a part of the war reparations and were used for storage on the northern side of Station Road.

With the return of peace, and after the Peace Celebrations held on 19 June 1919, life in Highworth took on its quiet pattern with little to disrupt the day to day life.

Although transport to Swindon improved with the provision of a motor bus service, so that the entertainment facilities of the town, in particular the cinema, became available, free time was short and money for entertainment scarce. As a result entertainment tended to be local and home produced with such institutions as concert parties, dances and whist drives not only providing entertainment, but also serving to raise funds for the voluntary organizations in the town.

However, two areas of life in the 1930s were of national interest, and as such provided interest and entertainment in the town. One of these was the royal

The King and Queen Hotel dressed for the Peace Celebrations

Celebrations for the Silver Jubilee of King George V and Queen Mary at Hannington

family, who during the period of the middle to late '30s provided the reasons for national celebration in the Silver Jubilee of King George V and Queen Mary in 1935, and the coronation of King George VI and Queen Elizabeth in 1937. For both of these celebrations Highworth was dressed overall, with a commemorative service in the parish church, celebration lunches, sports days, bonfires etc. However, these two occasions of national celebration were punctuated by national sadness at the death of King George V on 20 January 1936, and the abdication of King Edward VIII on 10 December of that year.

The other national interest of the time was provided by the fascination of flight, although the incidence of seeing aeroplanes in flight was increasing in Highworth, particularly as the RAF had a number of stations within some twenty miles of the town and its planes were occasionally seen in flight. However, a closer involvement with aircraft was a more unusual occurrence, and one to still evince great interest and excitement. Such interest was provided on 1 October 1930 by the sight of the R.101 airship on its final proving flight before its fatal crash near Beauvais in France on 7 October on its projected flight to India, with the death of fifty-four.

A more intimate involvement with the aeroplane was provided by the occasional visit to a field, off the Coleshill road, of the Berkshire Aviation Tours Limited of East Hanney who besides providing short 'joy rides' at five shillings a time, also gave a 'barnstorming' display of aerobatics, using planes which had been surplus to the requirements of the RAF at the end of the war.

A significant local interest in flight was also provided by Teddy Elwell – son of Edward Elwell the local solicitor of Quarry House, Cricklade Road – who when visiting his father used to land his BAC Drone light plane in one of

A BAC Drone single-seat aeroplane of the type flown by Teddy Elwell

21

New Council Houses in Cherry Orchard

John Couling's fields at Swanborough next to the Freke Arms public house, and in the process produced an exodus of Highworthians to witness the scene. Later, as a wartime member of the RAF, Teddy Elwell would sometimes circle his father's house in his Supermarine Spitfire.

During this period Highworth grew slowly, most of the development being in the building of the so-called 'Council Houses' as a result of the Addison Council Housing Act of 1919. The earliest developments were of Park Avenue in 1925 and Cherry Orchard in 1927, and the last of the pre-war council housing was the building of King's Avenue in 1936 on the site of the old Bailey's Piece Cottages which were demolished to provide space for the development.

The influence of central government upon the residents of Highworth during this period was relatively slight, except in the succession of General Elections during the 1920s and 1930s. Highworth's reputation for lively elections most certainly pre-dates the 1918 Representation of the People Act, which effectively enshrined universal suffrage. As early as 1874 Daniel Gooch described the election campaign by saying 'On Friday I went to Highworth and a meeting there, which was well attended and the church bells even ringing on the occasion (a thing I was assured had never been done before). This Highworth had always been a dreadfully radical place.' A reputation which continued through the '20s, with the lighting of bonfires from the barrels of tar left by the roadside for road repairs, and even into the '30s with

Wendell Wakefield, an English Rugby International, demonstrating a rugby tackle on the platform of the old Board School, the then Infants School.

The later years of the 1930s saw Highworth gain some degree of national fame in the areas of education and sport, with the formation of a 'Strike School' (q.v.) in August 1937 as a protest against the implementation of the Hadow Report in the Highworth/Stratton St Margaret area, and the fame of John Mapson of Swindon Street playing for Sunderland FC versus Preston North End FC in the Association Football Cup Final at Wembley Stadium in April 1938.

Additionally these years saw the prospect of war growing ever closer. The passing of the Air Raid Precaution Act by Parliament in 1937 meant that the framework for the ARP services began to be laid down, and with the threat of poison gas being used in any future war the trial fitting of civilian gas masks was carried out in the Church Room, and somewhat later the local Boy Scouts were responsible for the assembly of these.

As relations with Germany further deteriorated, culminating in the crisis of the Munich settlement in September 1938, and the fear of imminent air attack on the country, precautions went as far as the digging of trenches in the Recreation Ground as shelter from feared aerial attack.

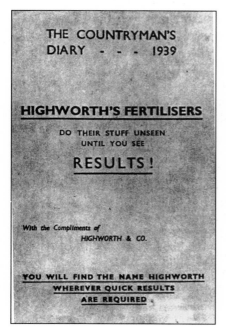

The cover of the 'Training Manual' for the Auxiliary Units at Coleshill House

Avro Cadet of Air Service Training of RAF Watchfield

The prospect of future war was further strengthened by the sight in the night sky of the searchlights of 63 Officer Cadet Training Unit, Royal Artillery, from the newly built Beckett Barracks at Shrivenham, as they prepared for their role in any future war.

A final harbinger of war affecting Highworth along with the rest of Britain was the conscription, for six months military training, of young men aged 20 to 21 on 27 April 1939, involving a number of Highworth's young men, who instead of serving their country for six months finally served for some six years.

CHAPTER THREE

September 1939 to 1960

The international events of late 1938 and early 1939, resulting in the German annexation of Austria in March 1938 and the occupation of the Czechoslovak Sudetenland in October, with Prime Minister Chamberlain's promise of 'peace in our time', were followed by the occupation of Bohemia and Moravia in March, together with further German demands in Lithuania and the Italian seizure of Albania in April 1939, leaving little doubt of the imminence of war. Already rearmament measures as a result of the Parliamentary decisions of 3 March 1936, when the defence budget leapt from £122 million to £158 million, were even beginning to influence the calm of Highworth. The building of 63 Officer Cadet Training Unit, Royal Artillery at Beckett Park, Shrivenham (presently the Royal Military College of Science) provided much needed employment in the various building trades which were suffering the effects of unemployment as a result of the 1930s depression. During the dark evenings the surrounding skies were lit by the searchlights of the cadets as they carried out their exercises.

The events of the recent Spanish Civil War, and in particular the destruction of Guernica from the air by the German Condor Legion, together with the predictions of H.G. Wells in his *War in the Air*, and the writings of the Italian Giulio Douhet who espoused the philosophy that future wars would be won from the air, led to an acute awareness of the need for an effective air raid precaution scheme. Semi-official figures estimated that in the first major air raid of any new war up to six hundred thousand people would be killed and twice that number injured. Thankfully these estimates turned out to be grossly exaggerated for any bombing raid throughout the war. However, such was the local fear of devastating raids that there was a strongly held belief that the new Upper Stratton Senior School (completed in 1936) was designed for use as a hospital when war broke out. Presumably the new style of architecture for the school had more in common in people's minds with a hospital than the schools in which they had been educated!

In order to produce an efficient Air Raid Precaution service, recruiting took place during the period of 1938–9 for Air Raid Wardens, First Aid, Auxiliary Fire Service and the Special Constabulary. Government publications on dealing with the problems of air raids were distributed to every household, and at least two sets of cigarette cards dealing with Air Raid Precautions were available to be collected, and so to provide further advice.

With the memory of poison gas warfare from the First World War still fresh in the minds of those in early middle age and older, considerable importance was attached to the provision of gas masks for all civilians as well as the armed services and ARP personnel. Fittings for these took place in the Church Room, and the Scout Troop was busily engaged in assembling civilian respirators in the games room of Redlands Court (kindly lent for the purpose by Mr Gerald Wilson).

The received intelligence concerning the expected raids was that besides heavy casualties there would be considerable disruption of the supply services, together with damage to the transport system. It was therefore felt necessary that stocks of emergency rations (corned beef and army style biscuits) should be laid down in each centre of population. Once again the Scout Troop was involved in the storage of these, in Highworth at a disused house next to Marsh's draper's shop, and in Stratton in disused garages at Stratton Park.

Parliament was recalled on 24 August and passed the Emergency Powers (Defence) Act, which empowered the Government to make such regulations as appeared necessary or expedient to secure public safety, the defence of the realm, the maintenance of public order, the efficient prosecution of the war, or the maintenance of supplies and services essential to life in the community. Also on the 24th, military and air force reservists were called up, and the ARP services were warned to stand ready.

With a further deterioration of the situation in Poland, plans for the evacuation of areas thought to be at a high risk of air raids (London, Manchester, Sheffield, etc.) were put into effect on 1 September. For this purpose the country had been divided into one of three classifications, evacuation, neutral or reception areas. Evacuation areas were as described, neutral areas were neither evacuated nor receiving evacuees, while reception areas such as Highworth, together with the remainder of Wiltshire, were to receive evacuees from the evacuation areas.

Highworth received its evacuees from Stratford in East London during the weekend of 1–3 September, and many were the traumas experienced during early September. Firstly the Stratford best known to the people of Highworth was that of Shakespeare – Stratford-upon-Avon, and certainly not part of the East End of London. Secondly the life styles of the evacuees and their hosts could not have been more different – the measured pace of life in Highworth, not greatly changed for generations, contrasted greatly with the mores and standards of inner-city life. While some evacuees made a happy transition, many did not, and many of their hosts were less than ecstatic about the situation, so that the billeting officers charged with making the Government's scheme work were presented with continuing problems.

Also on the night of 1 September, 'blackout' regulations came into force, and were to remain in force until 17 September 1944, when the threat of air raids had almost totally diminished, when it was replaced by a 'dim out'. The responsibility of monitoring the 'blackout' rested with the police and the Air Raid Wardens; even the humble garden bonfire was banned after dusk! In essence the blackout turned the familiar streets of Highworth into an after dusk obstacle course, despite the liberal use of white paint eventually applied to kerb-stones, lamp posts, telegraph poles, etc. in an attempt to make the lot of both pedestrians and motorists somewhat easier. The motorists, with their headlights shielded allowing only a narrow beam of light to illuminate the road, had particular difficulties, and in September 1939 the total of people killed in road accidents increased by nearly 100 per cent. A Gallup Poll published in January 1940 showed that about one person in five could claim to have sustained some injury as a result of the blackout – not serious in most cases, but it was painful enough to walk into trees, or fall over a kerb!

To most people the Declaration of War by the Prime Minister Neville Chamberlain at 11.15 a.m. on Sunday 3 September came as something of a relief after the indecision of the previous days. For example on 31 August only one person in five admitted to Mass Observation that he or she expected war.

However, the most immediate effect of the Declaration of War was the cancellation of all normal radio programmes and their replacement by regular news bulletins. Announcements included that 'all places of entertainment will be closed until further notice', and that 'schools were to be closed for at least a further week'. From late afternoon the main preoccupation of people in Highworth was with the convoys of coaches carrying Army reservists and Territorials from the Midlands to army camps on Salisbury Plain, and in the case of the Warwickshire Regiment to be billeted in Swindon. At this time and for most of the war years no troops were billeted in Highworth.

Besides the blackout there were other immediate changes in life in Highworth; the threat of air raids was still in the forefront of people's minds, and once again slit trenches were started in the Recreation Ground to provide shelter in the event of an air raid on the town, but with the threat never materializing these quickly became redundant. However, of more lasting influence was the reduction of bus services to and from Swindon. Rather than the regular hourly service, commencing at 7.15 a.m. from Highworth and continuing until the 8.45 p.m. from Swindon, this was immediately reduced to a two-hourly service, beginning from Highworth at 8.15 a.m. and continuing until the 7.45 p.m. from Swindon. Although this reduction was relatively short-lived, it caused considerable problems for those who used the bus service for travel to Swindon for either work or business. Similarly the closing of places of entertainment was equally short-lived, and by Christmas 1939 it was fairly obvious that the 'phoney' war was with us, with only the blackout and the rationing of petrol which had been introduced on 22 September still in effect. With no air raids on London or other centres of population the number of evacuees in Highworth and other reception areas was dwindling rapidly.

There were however some rather more permanent innovations as a result of the war: the regular collection on Saturday mornings of waste paper from houses and shops by the local Scout Troop, and town collections to provide comforts for those Highworth men who were serving with the Royal Navy, the Army or the Air Force.

The old Infants School between the Swindon and Shrivenham roads, closed as a result of the re-organization of education in the Highworth/Stratton St Margaret area in August 1937, had been developed as a First Aid and Light Rescue Post, complete with air locks at the doorways to prevent the entry of poison gas in the event of its use during an air raid. The old classroom on the Shrivenham road side carried on its walls an admonition 'to remove all your clothes, and place them in the dustbin' in the event of a mustard gas raid. This instruction remained in place for the next forty or so years and caused

The old Infants School used as the First Aid and Light Rescue Post. One of the garages for ambulances can be seen on the extreme right

considerable amusement to visitors when the building was in use as an antiques centre. While the Air Raid Precautions used the school, the Auxiliary Fire Service was based in the garages at Redlands Court, and Highworth had its own fire brigade again after some thirty years. So that these services might function efficiently in the event of an air raid, regular exercises were staged on Sunday mornings, stressing the co-operation of not only Highworth services, but also those of other areas involved.

On 29 September a National Registration Census was conducted recording the particulars of every citizen, and this was followed by the issue of a National Registration Identity Card containing the holder's name, address and National Registration number, which was to be carried at all times and produced upon demand by the police or armed services. Also issued in October were the first ration books, although these did not come into use until Monday 8 January, when the rations were 4oz bacon or ham, 12oz of sugar and 4oz of butter per week. Meat rationing, which was to begin in March 1940, consisted of meat to the value of 1s. 10d. per week. The ration book was to remain as a feature of British life until the early 1950s.

On the first day of the war Parliament had passed the National Service (Armed Forces) Act, under which all men between eighteen and forty-one were made liable for conscription. Registration for those aged from twenty to twenty-three commenced on 21 October, so that by the end of 1939 the first of the young men in these age groups had been conscripted into the Armed Forces, together with those who had volunteered for service. In contrast with the First World War there was no overwhelming rush of volunteers, as had occurred with patriotic fervour in the autumn of 1914, presumably because the mechanism for conscription already existed. Many of the volunteers tended to be for high profile tasks such as air crew in the RAF.

This process, which began slowly by removing young men from civilian life, continued inexorably until by June 1941 men aged forty were required to register, with the result that the whole town was shocked when later in the year Ivor Hawkins, the verger of St Michael's church, was conscripted into the Royal Air Force when in his forties.

For those remaining in the UK the winter of 1939–40 was marked by a spell of extremely hard weather, with heavy snow and freezing temperatures. Freezing rain, which coated roads, trees, etc. with a layer of ice, made travel virtually impossible and brought down telephone and electric power wires, with the resultant loss of heat, light and communication. Locally this inclement weather caused the fall of many of the elm trees in the avenues flanking Friar's Hill and Hangman's Elms, so aiding the fuel supplies of many families in the town.

Further changes to the pre-war routine were affected by the blackout, which caused evensong at St Michael's church to be held during the afternoons of the autumn and winter, as there was no possible way in which the church could be effectively blacked out. The parish church was further affected by the removal, for safe keeping in the event of air raids, of the recently installed east window.

The normal routine of the town was further changed by the sharing of the Council School (now Southfields Junior School) by evacuated schools from Stratford, and even with the use of the British School a system of part-time schooling had to be introduced. In the independent sector of education both Eastrop Grange and Warneford Place made their buildings available to act as hosts for girls' boarding schools evacuated from the danger areas around London. The early experience of the boredom of the 'phoney' war was relieved when one of the barrage balloons, which had been provided at the outbreak of war for the low-level defence of Swindon, broke free from its moorings and carried on the prevailing wind eventually came to rest with its cable entwined in the tower of St Leonard's church, Stanton Fitzwarren.

The winter of 1939–40 brought one permanent change to the area, namely the development of a shadow factory and airfield between Stanton and South Marston for Phillip and Powis Aircraft Ltd of Woodley near Reading. Phillip

Aerial view of the Phillip and Powis aircraft factory under construction at South Marston

and Powis were currently involved in the production of the Miles Master III, a single-engined advanced trainer essential for the training of the pilots of the Hurricane and Spitfires which were later to contest the Battle of Britain.

The building of the factory brought much needed employment to the area (there being still more than one million unemployed at the time of Dunkirk in May 1940, the figure having risen due to the exceptionally bad winter weather), but this also caused some dissatisfaction due to the high rates of pay being offered. The factory in common with all other shadow factories was built on the 'time and materials plus' basis of costing, so that 'tea boys' on the site were frequently paid more than skilled workers in other trades in the area. Once completed, the factory was eager to seek skilled workers, and the high rates of pay together with frequent overtime made jobs in the factory highly sought after.

The spring of 1940 passed without any great changes in Highworth's way of life, which adjusted to such inconveniences as rationing, 'call-up', blackout, etc., but the invasion of Norway and Denmark followed shortly by the 'Blitzkrieg' in the west with the invasion of France and the Low Countries soon changed all that. The evacuation from Dunkirk and the fall of France brought the nearness of the war home to everyone, and for the first time troops were stationed in Highworth. A detachment of the Royal Army Services Corps was encamped for a short while in The Park until a more permanent camp was available elsewhere. The Market Square was pressed into use as a barrack square for their drill and arms drill parades, attracting an appreciative crowd of spectators for whom it provided a welcome distraction from the sameness of day to day life.

This period of 1940 became one of great change and tense excitement, with the German forces poised on the coast of France and the invasion of England considered both imminent and inevitable. With the army having suffered considerable losses of both men and material in France, the situation facing the country was parlous in the extreme.

In an attempt to address this situation Anthony Eden, Secretary for War, made a broadcast to the nation on the evening of 14 May in which he explained that the German success in Belgium and Holland had shown how dangerous parachute attack might be to Britain itself.

He went on: 'Since the war began, the Government has received countless inquiries from all over the kingdom, from men of all ages, who are for one reason or another not at present engaged in military service and who wish to do something for the defence of the country. Now is the opportunity. We want large numbers of such men in Great Britain who are British subjects, between the ages of fifteen and sixty-five to come forward now and offer their services in order to make assurance double sure. The name of the new force which is now to be raised will be the "Local Defence Volunteers".'

Police stations throughout the country were besieged by men of all ages anxious to serve their country in its moment of danger. Within a few days of Eden's broadcast, the 9th Battalion, which included the Highworth Company under the command of Major Van de Weyer of South Marston and had platoons at Highworth, South Marston, Stratton, Hannington and Castle Eaton, was 1,000 strong. Early drill parades took place on the playground of the Council School (Southfields Junior School), providing an attraction for the local youth and a popular source of entertainment. Eventually the Highworth Company became designated as 'D' Company under the command of Major Sir T. Noel Arkell, with its headquarters in the Young Men's Institute in Sturgess's Alley (presently the Highworth Council Offices) and using the church tower for observation, a throwback to the situation which prevailed during the Civil War.

The operational role of LDV (later the Home Guard) was not agreed for some months, causing considerable anxiety. The LDV was by now a national force, one and three quarter million strong, yet had no uniforms or arms available to it, although the enemy was at the door.

After the perceived experience of the German 'Blitzkrieg' in France and the Low Countries, the first danger appeared to be from the so-called 'Fifth Columnists', so that from 31 May road-blocks were erected on all main roads throughout the country, and all traffic was stopped and checked from an hour before sunset to an hour after dawn. This went on for some weeks, then the number of road-blocks was reduced and eventually removed entirely, but not before there had been some 'incidents' − fortunately none serious. Initially these road-blocks around Highworth were made from whatever materials were available; eventually these were replaced by 'dragon's teeth' made from old railway rails, which dropped into sockets set in the road. Evidence of these can still be seen when 'road planing' takes place before re-surfacing of the roads leading into the town: at the top of Lechlade Hill, in Swindon Road outside the old Board School and outside Westrop Cottage in Cricklade Road. One of the very few reminders of the war remaining in the town is the steel hook set into the wall outside Westrop Cottage; local folk-lore has it that this was used to stretch a steel wire across the road to decapitate German troops attacking along the Cricklade Road. More prosaically the hook was used for attaching a 'concertina' barbed wire entanglement as part of the road-block at this point.

Eventually the role of the 9th Battalion of the now Wiltshire Home Guard became to deny the enemy free passage through the Battalion area. For this purpose Highworth, being a centre of communication, was designated a centre of resistance through which no enemy was to be allowed to pass, and was to form in depth part of the so-called General Headquarters Line of

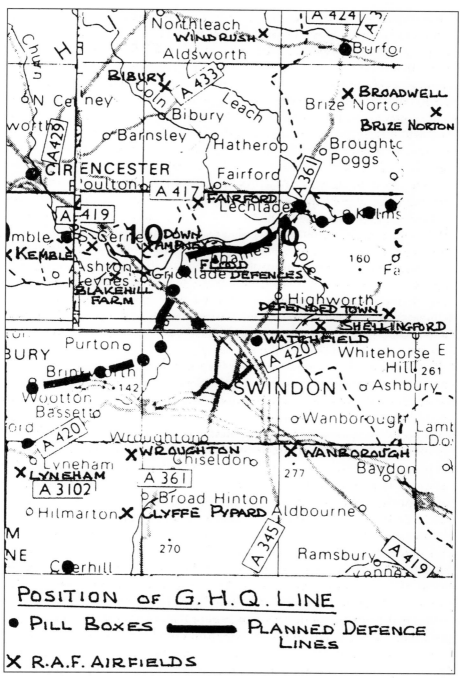

GHQ Line and RAF stations

defence, which in this area consisted of pill boxes along the River Thames and the Thames and Severn Canal together with anti-tank traps at Seven Bridges on the Swindon to Cirencester road at Blunsdon station on the old pack horse route through Blunsdon to Purton, and at Castle Eaton the flooding of the meadows alongside the River Thames (see p. 33). This line of defence was planned to resist any German advance into the Midlands after a break-out from their bridgeheads. These defence works, mostly still *in situ*, represent prime examples of Second World War military archaeology. German plans for 'Operation Sealion', which were captured at the end of the war, clearly show the intention of such a drive to the Swindon area. (See *Invasion* by Kenneth Macksey, Greenhill Books, London 1980; *Invasion of England 1940* by Schenk, Conway Press, London 1990). To this end many exercises were carried out with the 1st Motor Training Battalion of the King's Royal Rifle Corps stationed at Chiseldon Camp and used as the 'enemy' in the Home Guard's defence exercises. Highworth assumed a considerable importance in the organization of the 9th Battalion, with its headquarters moving to the King and Queen Hotel on 16 February 1942. It is not the place of this chapter to dwell too long on the story of the Home Guard despite its considerable importance and involvement in the war; readers who desire a more detailed study are referred to Major Mackay's *The History of the Wiltshire Home Guard* (1946).

Throughout this period of 1940 the countryside around Highworth assumed a new appearance. The threat of airborne, parachute and glider borne landings from the Luftwaffe's Junkers 52/3m troop carriers and DFS 230 gliders after their use during the campaign in the Low Countries led to many of the larger fields being obstructed by such means as poles set in the ground, old farm machinery, etc. in an attempt to deter such landings.

Furthermore the immediate threat of invasion provided a new role for Coleshill House and its estate, and so indirectly for Highworth, and in particular for Mrs Mabel Stranks, sub-postmistress for Highworth, who acted as intermediary in all postings to the school of resistance training at Coleshill House from the Highworth sub-post office in High Street (presently Vicraian – hairdressers, and The Flower Basket florists). The role of GHQ Auxiliary Units was to prepare selected members of the Armed Forces and the Home Guard to lead small units whose duties in the event of an invasion were to remain in the mainly coastal areas behind the invading German troops and to carry out a form of guerilla warfare behind the enemy lines, similar to that carried out later by the various Resistance groups on the continent of Europe. To this end the men selected were those whose skills made them intimately familiar with the country in which they would have fought, and despite the shortage of arms and equipment the Auxiliary Units had top

Coleshill House, headquarters for the training of the Auxiliary Units

priority in all things, with new weapons being provided for them before the conventional forces saw them.

All postings to GHQ Auxiliary Units in Coleshill House were made c/o GPO Highworth, Wiltshire, and those who had the temerity to query their postings to a post office were told 'why not go to the one in Highworth and see what happens?' Mrs Stranks after seeking proof of their identity would telephone Coleshill House saying, 'Some more of your lot are down here', and telling the new arrivals, 'Somebody's coming to fetch you!'

Another local country house was involved in the organization of the Auxiliary Units; at Hannington Hall were housed the ATS signallers whose task was to maintain communications between the various sections. To maintain the essential secrecy the cover name of 'Special Duties Section' was bestowed upon them.

As with all secret organizations rumours concerning the activities at Coleshill House abound, although at the time very little was known of these happenings. Certainly there were explosions occurring within the estate at unusual hours, and it seemed rather odd that there should be a Royal Artillery anti-aircraft emplacement – albeit only armed with a Lewis gun – at the foot of Badbury Hill; but strange and apparently unaccountable happenings were fairly commonplace throughout the war. On a personal note my maternal grandfather had until a few years before been gamekeeper on the estate, and he most certainly was unaware of the type of activity there.

It is also germane to make the point that despite claims to the contrary no locals feature in the list of Auxiliary Units group leaders. This is hardly surprising in view of the fact that these units were intended to operate in the areas of the enemy beachheads and not in central southern England, where, had the invading Germans succeeded, the battle would have been more mobile.

Those who wish to know more of the Auxiliary Units are referred to *The Last Ditch* by Lampe, Cassell (1968) and 'Front Line County', *Kent at War* by Rootes, Hale (1980).

By mid-1940 the number of airfields within a ten-mile radius of Highworth (five minutes flying time for most of the planes involved) was obvious from the amount of aerial activity over the town. On all but days of the worst weather the aeroplane spotter would see the Airspeed Oxford twin engine trainer from RAF South Cerney, from Brize Norton more Oxfords, and the raucously noisy North American Harvard single-engined advanced trainer. The nearest of the airfields, RAF Watchfield, developed from a small pre-war training field and provided more Airspeed Oxfords together with the Avro Anson which were in use there at the Blind Approach Training and Development Unit. Watchfield's contribution to the winning of the war is impossible to assess, but it certainly played an important part in improving the safe return of many an operational crew. In the early days Watchfield was also host to the Avro Cadets of Air Service Training, Hamble, still in their dark green civil livery. The Cadets had been forced to leave Southampton Water by the unwelcome attention of the Luftwaffe in the early days of the Battle of Britain. Eventually the Cadets removed to RAF Shellingford, where they were replaced by the De Havilland Tiger Moth – initial trainers which became renowned for flying alongside the main Swindon to Paddington railway line at the same speed as the train, hence appearing to the passengers to be stationary! A further trick of the instructors was to use the wheels of their Tiger Moths to gently upend Women's Land Army Girls who were busy hoeing in the surrounding arable fields.

The early stages of the Battle of Britain saw a number of these local airfields come under attack by the Luftwaffe. On Friday 16 August, RAF Brize Norton was attacked by two Junkers 88 twin-engined medium bombers. The raid, which lasted half-a-minute, proved to be the most spectacular attack on any British airfield during the war. Around thirty small high explosive bombs and a few incendiaries were dropped. They were sufficient to destroy two hangars and to kill fourteen individuals as well as destroy forty-six aircraft (most of which were in their hangars with petrol tanks filled for Monday's flying). There was widespread blast damage and not until darkness fell were all fires out. The resulting conflagration was clearly visible from Highworth as the author can testify.

On the following Sunday RAF Windrush (a training station some four miles west of Burford) was attacked by a Heinkel III, a twin-engined heavy bomber, which in the process was rammed by an Avro Anson from the station, with both aircraft crashing in flames. On the next day RAF Bibury, which accommodated Supermarine Spitfires from RAF Exeter on night standby, was attacked by Junkers 88 which caused some damage, one airman killed, and the destruction of two Spitfires.

Among other relatively local airfields attacked during the period of the Battle of Britain was RAF Kemble, which was attacked in July, October and November resulting in many of the aircraft held in the Maintenance Unit there being transferred to RAF Watchfield, where they were dispersed around the perimeter of the station. Most of these aircraft were Hawker Hart (single engine, biplane, light bombers) variants, which were shortly to be pressed into service as glider tugs at stations such as RAF Brize Norton when the decision was taken to develop glider-borne forces.

However, a few days earlier (Thursday 15 August) the Short Brothers aircraft factory at Rochester in Kent had been attacked by Dornier 17 twin-engined medium bombers of Kampfgruppe 3, causing very considerable damage and the destruction of the recently completed Short Stirling four-engined bombers. This attack was to have considerable influence on activities in the Highworth area as construction of the Short Stirling was transferred nearby. A 'shadow' factory at South Marston, originally intended for an extension of the Phillip and Powis factory, together with newly built 'shadow' factories at Sevenhampton and Blunsdon combined with 24 shop of the GWR factory in Swindon were to be utilized in the construction of the Stirling. So that flight tests of the Stirling could take place from the South Marston airfield it was necessary to lay down concrete runways to accept the very considerable weight of the Stirling.

The local roads presented certain problems in the movement of completed fuselages from the factory at Sevenhampton to the flight sheds at South Marston for final assembly. The direct road from Sevenhampton to South Marston was impassable to the 'Queen Mary' vehicles which carried the 87 ft long fuselages. As a result these were brought along the Shrivenham road to Highworth, but experiencing some considerable difficulty in negotiating the corner by the First Aid Post into Swindon Road. A police motor-cycle escort was required along the narrow winding road through South Marston to the flight sheds.

Police holding up traffic in South Marston to allow passage of a Short Stirling fuselage

Fuselage of a Short Stirling negotiating the narrow roads of the district

Although the area was subject to many air raid warnings during this period, there were no raids directly upon the Highworth district. However, for one night in particular Highworth lay immediately under the flight path of the German bombers. The night in question was that of Thursday 14 November, the night of the infamous raid on Coventry. Highworth lay directly under the German approach beam, 'Wesser', which guided the Heinkel IIIs of Kampfgruppe 100 from Vannes about 150 miles south of Cherbourg to their targets at Coventry. Kampfgruppe 100 was a pathfinder unit for the Luftwaffe. Their first aircraft were passing over Highworth by 7 p.m.; the raid continued until the early hours of the morning and the aircraft returned by a similar flight path, so that Highworth was overflown by the Luftwaffe for a period of some seven hours.

The presence of German aircraft over Highworth was no new phenomenon, as Swindon was one of the turning points in the Luftwaffe's 'X System' of blind bombing developed by Kampfgruppe 100 during the early years of the war. The great difference on this occasion was the duration of the raid, and the obvious intensity of the attack.

More mundane, but leaving a permanent mark on the town, was the collection of iron railings, a move brought about by the temporary shortage of iron ore as a result of the Norwegian campaign. Initially this process was voluntary, but later these were removed compulsorily, the criteria for the railings to remain being their architectural significance or their requirement for purposes of safety. In Highworth the railings surrounding the churchyard, cemetery and many private houses were sacrificed for the war effort and the manufacture of armaments. Spared however were those surrounding Inigo House and the archway to the Congregational (United Reform) church. Old photographs of the town show the difference the railings made to the look of Highworth. However there appears to be some considerable doubt as to whether or not such collections aided the war effort, but the psychological impact at the time was the important factor.

February 1941 saw a 'stick' of high explosive and incendiary bombs which were dropped between RAF Watchfield and Highworth, presumably aimed at the former. The area bombed extended from Highmoor Copse, very narrowly missing Eastrop, to what is now the Haresfield Estate, with the incendiary bombs landing in the gardens of Cherry Orchard. Later in the year a single high explosive bomb was dropped alongside the footpath to Stanton Fitzwarren, through Botany Fields near the old water tower; but this failed to explode and was excavated from the underlying Oxford Clay by a Royal Engineer bomb disposal squad, and safely detonated.

By this time the 'shadow' factories at Sevenhampton, Blunsdon and South Marston were ready, with many of the machine tools having been moved from Rochester to South Marston, and production of the Short Stirling

The Congregational church before the removal
of the iron railings to assist the war effort

re-commenced with staff transferred from Rochester or recruited locally.
Many of these were young women who had registered for war work and who
had been trained in engineering skills at the Technical College, Swindon.

Although production of the Stirling was set back by more than a year a
total of 353 Stirlings were eventually built at South Marston.

The shortage of accommodation for this influx of workers resulted in a
change in the appearance of Highworth which lasted for over twenty years.
To accommodate these immigrant aircraft workers and their families special
estates of Ministry of Aircraft Production bungalows were built locally at
Kingsdown and in Highworth on Niblett's chicken farm at Westrop Farm
between Station Road and Westrop. These brick built bungalows with
corrugated asbestos roofs, hot water systems and bathrooms were a
considerable improvement on many of the unmodernized cottages in the
town, and represented an appreciable addition to the housing stock of
Highworth. Rivers Road, Newburgh Road and Newburgh Crescent were to
play a not inconsiderable part in the war effort, but were also invaluable to the
Highworth Rural District Council in the post-war period. The MAP
bungalows as they became known were demolished in the '60s to make room
for the Home Farm development, and regrettably all that remains is the
memory, and the name commemorated in Newburgh House.

These mid-years of the war saw a fairly settled lifestyle developing, highlighted locally by the annual War Weapons Weeks, beginning in 1941, followed in 1942 by a 'Warship Week', in 1943 by 'Wings for Victory', and for the Second Front – Invasion of Europe – the 1944 celebration was 'Salute the Soldier'. These National Savings campaigns were celebrated with parades, church services and so on; besides providing an impetus for saving, they also provided highlights in an otherwise rather grey war-time existence. Civilian morale was to become as important to the war effort as that of the fighting services.

To this end civilian entertainment was vital, and in Highworth the British School was pressed into use as a once-weekly cinema, so providing some entertainment without having to venture into Swindon.

Fortunately there were very few crashes of RAF planes in the immediate area of Highworth. Sadly, however, four such crashes come to mind: that of an Airspeed Oxford from Watchfield at Hampton (presumably a malfunction of the Blind Approach System); an Avro Anson at Hannington; an Airspeed Horsa troop-carrying glider which crashed onto the railway line at the 'Butts'

A Short Stirling rolls out ready for a flight test

in late 1943. However, the most serious crash was that of an Avro Lancaster ED 381 of No. 1656 Heavy Conversion Unit which had been involved in a raid on the Ruhr, and on attempting to land at Brize Norton collided with a Vickers Wellington BJ 845, crashing at Wickstead Farm on the Coleshill Road. The Highworth Auxiliary Fire Service was called into action in the early hours of 17 June 1943 to deal with the resulting fire, and retrieve the bodies of the crew.

By early 1943 the influence of the United States on the war in Europe was becoming noticeable. By now Shrivenham had become an American base, and in the grounds of Hannington Hall some 2,000 coloured American troops were encamped. At this time, as throughout the war, the American forces were rigidly segregated, and the public houses of Highworth were convenient and popular visiting places for the GIs from both camps. Eventually after a series of unfortunate fracas at some of the town's hostelries, the town was patrolled by six pairs (one white, one coloured) of American Military Police – known colloquially as 'Snowdrops' on account of their white steel helmets and white cravats setting off their immaculate uniforms – who dealt in a most unceremonious manner with any breaches of discipline in the town. A further influence of the American presence in the area was their practice of ferrying into the various camps young women from the surrounding area to act as partners for the GIs at the dances arranged. This led to a familiarity with the latest American dance craze of 'Jitterbug', and to an appreciable number of marriages, and the coining of the term 'GI Bride'.

During 1943 RAF Brize Norton had been concerned with the training of the crews of Armstrong Whitworth Albemarle twin-engined glider tugs, and Airspeed Horsa troop-carrying gliders in readiness for airborne operations against the mainland of Europe, with these combinations constantly overflying Highworth. By early 1944 RAF stations at Down Ampney, Broadwell (near Burford) and Fairford were also in the process of training glider crews, so that the sight of gliders and their tugs around Highworth was commonplace. In the case of RAF Fairford the tugs for the Horsas were provided by the Short Stirling which had now been replaced as a front-line bomber, and these combinations provided great interest for local youths who attempted to track down the tow ropes dropped in the fields between the airfield and Highworth.

These preparations represented only part of those for the 'Second Front' which were observable from Highworth. As the year developed the sight of convoys of arms and armour moving south along the A361 to the assembly areas in Hampshire, Dorset and Salisbury Plain became a common sight to the inhabitants of the town, and an appreciably more buoyant air became evident in the country.

Evidence of the nearness of a landing in Europe was provided to the people of Highworth one Sunday evening in late April when coming in from the west was a mass of troop-carrying planes, mainly American Douglas Dakota twin-engined troop carriers in use by the RAF on lend/lease. This in itself was not a surprising sight, but as the planes flew east over Highworth the sky was suddenly filled by billowing parachutes. Paratroopers were landing in large numbers in the triangle formed by Highworth, Coleshill and Buscot. Many of the townspeople were rushing on foot or on cycle to watch the landing, and to see such novelties as folding bicycles, motorized scooters, folding carts, etc., dropped with the troops. As well as providing a sensational sight, and great interest and excitement, the exercise also provided a considerable supply of silk from the parachute canopies for local seamstresses. The importance of this particular exercise was not at that time clear to the residents of Highworth, but the publication by HMSO of *By Air to Battle – The Official Account of the British Airborne Divisions*, which describes the vital attack on the bridges over the Caen Canal and the River Orme, explains the event. Training for this very difficult and dangerous operation began in April, and Chatterton, in command of the Glider Pilot Regiment, was fortunate enough to discover a part of England, bounded roughly by the four villages of Aston, Bampton, Buckland and Hinton, which is very much like that part of Normandy where the two bridges were situated. The area was heavily hedged as was the bocage country of the area under attack. 'Some weeks before the show we did an exercise' reports Major R.J. Howard DSO who led the attack on the swing-bridge over the Caen Canal, 'during which we "pranged" the bridges at Lechlade. This was a tremendous help, for the place was very like the part of Normandy we subsequently attacked.'

'D' Day, Monday 6 June 1944, was presaged in Highworth by the unforgettable sight on the Sunday evening of columns of Albemarles towing Horsa gliders from 295 and 570 Squadrons of No 38 Group from RAF Hanwell, wearing their black and white invasion stripes, along with American C.47 troop carriers similarly marked from Membury and Ramsbury flying north to gain height before setting course for Normandy from the tower of St Michael's church. The news on the next morning of 'Operation Overlord', the invasion of mainland Europe and the opening of a 'second front', came as no surprise to the residents of Highworth.

During the summer of 1944 Highworth was once again directly involved with the war. In June and July the town, along with many others in safe areas, received a number of evacuees from the south-east which was suffering attack from the first of the German's Vergeltungswaffe 1 (Vengeance Weapon 1), the pilotless bomb known colloquially as the 'Doodlebug'; the area of Metropolitan Kent which bore the brunt of much of the early attack being known as 'Doodlebug Alley'.

The 17th September saw the beginning of the airborne landing at Arnhem; on this day, and the two following, 10,000 troops of the 1st Airborne Division were air-landed in the vicinity of Arnhem, using aircraft and gliders from Fairford, Broadwell, Down Ampney, Brize Norton and Blakehill. During the course of the battle of Arnhem, and the advance of the British 1st Army, the re-supply situation became highly critical with the result that a re-supply operation code-named 'Market' was set up in which Highworth played an essential part.

To this end No 4 Supply Reserve Depot, Royal Army Service Corps at the Old Powder Works, in Gypsy Lane, Swindon, provided the supplies, which were to be airlifted from the RAF stations originally involved in the airlift of the Airborne Division. The vital link in this re-supply operation was to 504 Company RASC, who were encamped in The Park, and their 3 tonner lorries lining Swindon Street were used to transport the supplies from 4 SRD to the various airfields. The operation lasted until 25 September, by when the 1st Airborne Division had either been forced to surrender, or in the case of some 1,700 men had escaped across the River Rhine.

By this time most of the launching sites of the V1s had been overrun by the advancing allied troops, and most of the evacuees were again able to return home.

The end of the war was now fairly clearly in sight, and the thoughts of the townspeople of Highworth could realistically turn to making the 'Welcome Home Fund' a reality, the result of which was the Community Centre in the Recreation Ground although it was not finally opened until 1965.

With the end of the war in August 1945 came a slow return to the normality of life in Highworth. Victory was finally celebrated on 8 June 1946 with church services, parades and festivities. Demobilization of those who had served during the war continued steadily, while the young men of the community were still conscripted for military service.

The post-war period saw a deteriorating economic situation throughout the country with recovery slow and patchy, at times not assisted by the vagaries of the weather. Highworth in common with most of the country suffered an extremely severe winter during 1946–7 resulting in power cuts, factories closed, etc. Locally the Shrivenham road was blocked with snow drifts up to ten feet deep making travel virtually impossible.

However, development occurred slowly; the advent of television in the late 1940s with its rash of 'H' aerials on roofs was accelerated by the wish to watch the coronation of Queen Elizabeth II, when once again Highworth along with the rest of the country was 'en fete'.

Development in Highworth remained slow with little house building; Orange Close and Quarry Crescent were the first of the post-war council houses.

Supermarine Spitfire 24s under construction at South Marston

Employment prospects remained much as pre-war, with Bartrop's and the mat factory providing most of the local employment, while the now British Rail factory still provided employment for many. In 1945 the Vickers-Supermarine aircraft company acquired the Phillip and Powis factory at South Marston for the production of Spitfire 24s and Seafires for the Royal Navy as well as for refurbishing Spitfire IXs for foreign air forces.

Production of Supermarine Attackers for the Royal Navy was followed by the Swift, the experimental Type 508, and eventually the Scimitar before the works closed. During the late '40s and the early '50s the speed of aircraft approached the speed of sound with the resulting 'sonic bang'. 'Sonic bangs' were therefore commonplace in the area with resultant complaints from angry market gardeners. Eventually legislation prevented the breaking of the sound barrier over land, so ending this problem.

Some twenty years after Highworth lost its older pupils the situation was resolved when the Warneford Secondary Modern School was opened in September 1957, and all Highworth pupils were able to attend school in the town.

CHAPTER FOUR

Education and Youth Organization

Education in any sense that would now be generally understood is essentially a twentieth-century phenomenon; in 1818, for example, only one in four children throughout England was receiving any kind of education at all, and half the adult population could not read or write their own names. However despite its relative modernity the strands of education in Highworth stretch back to the early seventeenth century. In common with most of Wiltshire's market towns no evidence exists of any foundation grammar school in Highworth. This was in contrast to the adjoining counties of Gloucestershire and Oxfordshire, where the provision of such schools was relatively more common. This is clear evidence of the relative poverty of much of Wiltshire, and of the north-eastern corner in particular.

However, in 1642 the Highworth churchwardens paid for repairs to a schoolhouse as follows:

To John Leader for his work over the School House £3 16s. 0d.

To John Leader for leades and solder in the schoolhouse £9 0s. 0d. paid of his bill.

Also on 3 May 1678 the churchwardens presented 'what is commonly called ye school house being out of repair and we require by ye Feast of St John [24 June] if that be possible.'

The school was run by Mr Dudley, a minister at Highworth.

Perhaps his most famous pupil was Narcissus Marsh who later became Archbishop of Armagh. C.B. Fry in his book *Hannington* tells us Narcissus was the son of William Marsh of Hannington.

Narcissus was born in 1638, the youngest of five children, all of whom received a good education. After attending schools in Hannington and Lushill, Narcissus went to Mr Dudley of Highworth where he first began to learn Latin. After attending two more local schools he went to Oxford, where he took a Bachelor of Arts degree in 1648. In later life he wrote that in all his early schools 'I never was so much as once whipt or beaten.' Narcissus Marsh became Archbishop of Armagh in 1703 and died in 1713. Evidently the

Highworth school continued through the seventeenth century because the parish baptisms book records that Richard Davies of Westrop was schoolmaster in 1705. Unfortunately not much more is known of this school.

Records however do exist in the parish registers of a charity school in the Vestry House. This free school for the poorer children of Highworth, Eastrop, Westrop, Hampton, Sevenhampton and South Marston (note the separation of Eastrop, Westrop and Hampton from Highworth itself – see Chapter 1) was largely the brainchild of James Ayescough and Henry Haggard who, in addition to being enthusiastic supporters of the school, acted as the initial collectors of funds. These in the summer of 1722 consisted of £43 8s. 9d. provided by some seventy-six subscribers, the most noticeable of whom were Henry Hore £5, Edmund Warneford £5, and Thomas Batson Davies £3, and a gift of £5 from William Greenaway and his wife for commutation of penance for antenuptial fornication. These funds were spent on the salary of a master for teaching, £30, and on other essentials.

From Christmas Day 1722 money for the Charity School was collected in church on the main feast days of the year. This so-called 'sacrament money' was collected in Highworth on Christmas Day, Epiphany, Good Friday, Easter Day, Whit Sunday and Trinity Sunday; while in Sevenhampton it was collected on 30 December and on Palm Sunday. The first of these collections amounted to £6 3s. $^{3}/_{4}$d and was used to buy bibles, Books of Common Prayer, catechisms, children's guides, paper, quills, besoms, chairs and forty caps and bands, which give some small indication of the approximate number of children involved.

During the next few years the income from sacrament money remained fairly constant, but the number of subscribers declined with the result that it was necessary to use sacrament money to maintain the salary of the master, the cost of materials for the school being met by the parents or the sponsors of pupils.

Until 1756 no rules had been specified for the school, but by this time income had declined and conditions had changed since 1722. However, the rules of the school indicate that it catered for rather more than fifty children at a cost of 8s. a year; moreover the parents or sponsors of each child were required to provide the necessary papers and equipment. However subscribers of small sums could combine and if the total reached 8s. they could then agree upon a child to be admitted to the school.

By 1775 the school's income had fallen sharply to £14 2s. 6d. from only twenty-four subscribers and was accompanied by a similar decline in sacrament money to £4 4s. 0d., which together with a dividend of £3 12s. 0d. from £120 in 3% Consols bequeathed by a Mr Triplet, and an annual gift of £1 12s. 0d. from the Revd Mr Buston, gave a total income of £23 10s. 6d. Clearly the master, a Mr Blagrove, had suffered a considerable decline in salary!

In ten years time conditions had changed yet again, and although the master's salary had now risen to £28 11s. 6d. the way in which it was raised had changed fairly dramatically. Voluntary contributions had declined to £6 18s. 6d. from ten subscribers, while sacrament money represented only £2 12s. 0d. Annual gifts similar to that of the Revd Mr Buston amounted to £13 14s. 0d. while income from capital bequeathed to the school provided £5 7s. 0d. a year; in addition to the gift of Mr Triplet there were further gifts of £100 in Consols from the Provident Society, £70 from Mr Buston and a gift from a Mr Davies which yielded £1 a year.

Inevitably the running of the Charity School was not without the occasional controversy. In 1790 William Blagrove, the schoolmaster, died in a smallpox epidemic that swept through Highworth causing eighty-one deaths in only a few months. John Lord was then appointed master by the unanimous decision of the Trustees, but he was moved to note that 'Because a certain party in this town could not make choice of the Master of the said School, withdrew their subscriptions . . .'. It would appear that some £9 14s. 0d. had been raised in 1789, but when John Lord was appointed master a number of subscribers immediately withdrew their support leaving only £6 11s. 0d. However this loss was more than made up later in the year when a Mrs Angell left a gift to make up a sum of £220 in 4% Consols – so that 'the Minister may appoint Sarah Crawford's children and any other of her poor relations who shall desire such assistance, to receive the benefit of the Charity School.'

By 1794 John Lord had left his post and Thomas Jenkinson was appointed to teach in the Charity School in his place. This too was a controversial appointment because two years later it was noted that 'We, the Vicar, Churchwardens, Overseer and Principal Inhabitants do not approve of Mr Thomas Jenkinson to teach the Charity School any longer and we do hereby appoint John Savoury . . .'.

At this time, and well into the nineteenth century, most children did not receive any regular schooling. For those children of poor families there were 'dame schools', which initially were set up by quite respectable women who charged a few pence for giving very basic lessons. These were often run by women who had little or no education themselves, and were certainly not competent to teach, and although a few attempted to teach basic subjects, many were little more than child-minders for very young children while their parents were at work. For example Cassey's *Directory of Berkshire and Oxfordshire with a portion of Wiltshire* for 1869 lists the following schools in Highworth: M.A. Burgess – ladies school, S. and E. Dore – ladies school, Westrop, Mrs E. Litten – school, Westrop.

For most of the nineteenth century, education remained voluntary; no child was forced to go to school except by its own choice.

During this period elementary education for working-class children developed largely through the schools provided by two voluntary societies – the British and Foreign School Society, founded in 1808, and The National Society for the Education of the Poor in the Principles of the Established Church, founded in 1811. Although ostensibly voluntary organizations, both Societies received increasing amounts of State aid in the form of annual grants. They had strong religious affiliations, the National (or Church) schools being as the title of the Society suggests closely connected to the Church of England, teaching religion according to its doctrines, while the British Schools had a Nonconformist bias.

In Highworth the British School in Brewery Street was commenced on 24 July 1849 with the foundation stone laid by a Mrs Plummer when 'A large multitude assembled to witness the proceedings, and our Sunday Schools and Day Schools, to the number of 200 children, were regaled with cake and tea.' Within four months of laying the foundation stone the British School was opened on 9 November having cost just under £300 to build.

The National School in Swindon Road was built between 1835 and 1855 taking over the Charity School in 1855, when the Vicar and Churchwardens appointed Henry Apted to the post of schoolmaster. According to the Post

Interior of the old National School (currently the Infants School), *c.* 1931

Office Directory of 1855 both the British School and the National School had separate infant schools, the National School and its Infant School being in Eastrop. This is almost certainly the building at the bottom of Eastrop Hill which has been in use by the Scouts since their formation in 1909. The move to the Swindon Road by the National School did not take place until the building was finished in 1855. Between 1835, when the schoolhouse was built, and 1855, when the school was completed, the National School seems to have used the premises of the old Charity School. The National School was further enlarged in 1866 to accommodate 400 pupils, before the appointment on 28 April 1894 of a School Board of five members to implement the legislation of the 1870 Elementary Education Act. Robert Elwell was clerk to the Board and Frederick Drew of Swindon Street was appointed as attendance officer at the princely salary of £10 per annum.

The Post Office Directory of 1855 mentions a ladies boarding school run by a Miss Burgess, a boarding school in Sheep Street run by Edward Dyke, and a preparatory school in Westrop run by Mrs Elizabeth Litten. In 1875 John Southwell was running a boarding and day school in the Vicarage House; at this time the vicar lived in West Hill House in Cricklade Road. During the 1890s Miss Thomas ran a very successful school at Lassington House, Swindon Street, advertisements claiming that this school was founded in 1830. It continued as a school until the 1930s when the Misses Gundry ran the school; in the early 1930s the author remembers borrowing books from the stock which had been used in the school by the Misses Gundry.

The Board School in Shrivenham Road, presently Southfields Junior School

By 1897 a new Board School for 360 children had been built in Shrivenham Road, with John Samuel Jenkins as master, and the original National School catering for those under seven years of age had Miss Annie Evans as mistress. The schools were always known vernacularly as the 'big' and 'little' schools respectively – presumably the labels applying to the size of the pupils, and not to the size of the school. The Log Book of the Highworth Board School provides an interesting insight into education at the turn of the century. The following being a small selection of the entries:

1896

21 April – Visit to the Vicar's – The Chairman of the Board – to report the great stench found in the vicinity of the classroom.
22 April – The schools were closed by order of the Medical Officer.

1898

7 March – When the boys were ringing the bell this morning it fell from top to bottom but fortunately no one was injured. I reported the matter immediately to the clerk . . . absolute necessity of having it fixed securely.
25 April – During the afternoon 139 children were absent owing to a circus being in town.
25 June – Visit by Her Majesty's Inspector. The new building (the present Southfield Primary School) is very good and suitable and presents a pleasing appearance. The children are very neat and orderly and though the staff has been insufficient throughout the year, the teachers have worked hard and the progress is highly creditable.

Numbers present in the morning:
Boys 126   Girls 135   Total = 261   Numbers on Books 276.

22 June – Mr Elwell – Clerk to the Board – called in school during the morning and desired me to inform the staff that they would not be paid this month in consequence of there not being a quorum at the Board Meeting held the previous evening.
24 October – Cautioned – at the request of the Board – the boys who had gone in Mrs Newport's field adjoining the playground after their football.

1899

2 June – My duties as Headmaster terminate today. I do so with the deepest

sorrow . . . I have simply done my duty and in doing so have unwittingly given offence to those in authority . . . The reason for my dismissal has never been given to me and have never yet had a hearing . . . I make entry therefore as a protest against the unfair and un-English way I have been treated by the persons at present forming 'the majority of the Board' who have deprived me of my position.

5 June – I, Henry Scotton commenced duty as Head Teacher this morning.

30 June – Was served this day with a summons to attend before the magistrates at Swindon on Thursday 6 July on a charge of assaulting Chas Allsopp whom I had caned for using disgusting language to a girl in his class on Wed 28 June. He received four stripes on the seat.

7 July – The summons brought against me by Mrs Allsopp was dismissed yesterday.

20 July – The Board passed the following resolution at their meeting on the 18th 'That having received Mr Scottons (sic) report as to the Chas Allsopp case, the Board approve the action taken by Mr Scotton and consider that he has not exceeded his duty. The Board hope that prompt steps will be taken by him as far as possible to stop all bad language in the school.'

In addition to the Board School Kelly's Directory of 1899 cites three other educational establishments, viz. Mrs Emily Attewell – girls school, Westrop Terrace; Jn Humphreys – private school, Swindon Street, and Miss Elizabeth Hannah Thomas – ladies school, Lassington House; together with Wm Hawkins – teacher of music, Westrop.

Two provisions in particular had discouraged the early provision of proper schools for working-class children. In the first place most poor parents did not believe that a formal education was necessary for children whom they expected to become unskilled workers like themselves. This feeling was shared by many of their social superiors, who feared that educating the lower classes might encourage them to question their social status. The second consideration was a very pressing economic one: the wages earned by most unskilled workers were so low that they had to be supplemented by sending their children to work at an early age. If these children were sent to school instead it meant the loss of vital income for the family.

One of the methods used for financing schools was that termed the 'Payment by Results' system, where part of the school's grant was dependent upon regular attendance; events in the town were frequently greater attractions than the dull routine of school. The opportunity of earning money by the many kinds of casual work available in the town and the surrounding farms – potato picking, crop weeding, harvesting, sheep-shearing, poultry plucking or beating for the shoot – was strong temptation to poor families, with some farmers and other employers openly encouraging truancy of this kind. An example is provided by an entry in the school Log Book for 29 September 1898 which reads 'G. Sloper of Westrop House – a member of the Board – visited the school for the first time . . . and made full enquiries about the irregularity of attendance. The reason assigned to him by Albert Drewell – Standard II [age 8+] – for two days absence was that he stopped at home to pick up potatoes.'

This problem was not singularly of the nineteenth century, but continued into my own school days in Highworth, and even into my own post-1948 teaching career with 'spud picking' during the Michaelmas term being a frequent cause of absence from school for those who lived on farms in the outlying villages.

Education in Highworth changed little during the early years of the twentieth century, even the Great War of 1914–18 had produced little effect. However the 1902 Education Act had enabled the State through the newly elected County Councils to step in and take control of local education from the various local School Boards, so that education in Highworth was now effectively controlled from Trowbridge. By 1923 the headmistress of the Infants (the 'little') School was a Mrs Abigail Hann, while the headmaster of the Council (the 'big') School was the legendary Ernest Atkinson Booth ('General' to all his pupils and their parents after the founder of the Salvation Army).

The boys of Standards V, VI and VII, with headmaster Ernest 'General' Booth (left) and senior master W.H. 'Pete' Gale (right)

Hannington School, which closed in 1926 with pupils transferred to Highworth

By 1926 however, the first of an increasing number of changes took place. The schools at the neighbouring villages of Hannington (built for sixty children, and with Miss Charlotte Farnworth as mistress), Inglesham (built in 1870 with Mrs Jane Kinch as mistress and an average attendance of only fifteen) and Stanton Fitzwarren (partly supported by the Trenchard family, and with Mrs Ellen Hasell as mistress) were closed and their pupils transferred to Highworth, thus effecting a financial saving for the County Council. Transport was provided in the form of bicycles for pupils over eleven years of age, while for those under this age transport by hire cars was provided, initially by Fred Edmonds of High Street and later by Johnny Owen of Swindon Street, at the expense of the County Education Committee.

In the early '30s provision was made for the pupils in Standards VI, VII and x–VII to be taught woodwork to the boys, and needlework and domestic science to the girls. To this end these older pupils were transported by coach to a centre at Gorse Hill School, Swindon, where the facilities for such subject teaching were provided, it not being deemed economic to provide such facilities for a school the size of the Highworth Council School.

While the education provision in Highworth changed little during this period, changes were taking place which although they did not influence the vast majority had a considerable impact upon the 'brighter' children in the town and district, opening up their way to higher education, and the prospect of university.

In 1891 the Swindon and North Wiltshire Technical Instruction Committee was formed to administer the Further Education Acts of 1889 and 1891; and in 1896 the Swindon and North Wiltshire Technical Institute opened in Victoria Road, Swindon, and included a day secondary school for boys. From 1897 the school began to admit girls, and scholarships awarded by the County Council enabled children in Highworth (and other areas outside Swindon) to attend. Previously, secondary education could only be obtained upon payment of fees at either Marlborough, Cirencester, Burford or King Alfred's, Wantage Grammar Schools with all the inherent problems of obtaining a place, and of travelling from Highworth each day or boarding.

The influence of the 'Tech' (as it was affectionately known long after its name was changed in 1926 to the College Secondary School) upon education in the area is difficult to measure but is none the less considerable and significant. The provision of secondary education in the area was further strengthened by the opening of the Euclid Street Central Higher Elementary School in 1904 (later Euclid Street Secondary School), and the Commonweal Secondary School in 1927.

Initially places at these secondary schools were obtained either by scholarship examination, or by the payment of fees; but in 1933 all places in these schools were opened to competitive examination, and fees were remitted upon a scale fixed in proportion to parents' income. This probably unique example of 'one hundred per cent special place entry' to the secondary schools produced some rather unexpected educational developments.

Parents of those unable to pass the entry examination but able to afford the fees were still able to attempt to gain entry for their children to the grammar schools mentioned earlier. For those unable to obtain places at grammar schools recourse was to Bath Road (Swindon) High School for boys, and to Clyde House School, St Katherine's School for girls, or Selwood House School.

For a few years in the immediate pre-war years Highworth could once again boast of a private school. In this case the Highworth House School – private boarding and day school for boys, which advertised 'Preparation for School Certificate and Matriculation Exams. Fees Moderate.' The Principal was G.S. Hogan, Esq. DSO and so the school was known locally as 'Hogan's Academy'. The relatively small number of boys wearing the green and scarlet caps of the school was a frequent sight around Highworth. However, the school was a victim of the harsh economic times and succumbed with no trace remaining save that of its advertisement in the Highworth Guide of the period.

Upper Stratton Senior School, the destination for Highworth children over eleven from August 1937

In this immediate pre-war period, education in Highworth hit the national headlines. During the educational year 1936–7 the Wiltshire Education Committee made plans to implement the Hadow Report of 1926 which recommended 'a clean break in the education of children between the ages of eleven and twelve'. The plan for Highworth was that a new senior school was to be built at Kingsdown to be known as the Upper Stratton Senior School to cater for pupils over the age of eleven from Highworth, South Marston, Blunsdon, Upper Stratton, Lower Stratton and Haydon Wick – although in the event no pupils from Haydon Wick ever attended Upper Stratton Senior School.

Feelings in Highworth ran high at news of this plan which was to be implemented at the beginning of the Michaelmas term 1937, and which required the closing of the Infants (the 'little') School with Miss Kirk the headmistress retiring and the retirement of 'General' Booth as headmaster of the Council (the 'big') School, which would become a five to eleven primary school with W.H. Gale ('Pete' to all his pupils and the present senior master) appointed as headmaster. As a result of this plan and considerable inefficiency upon the part of the Wiltshire Education Committee a series of protest meetings was held in the town.

The outcome of these was that a 'Strike' school would be established in the town, using the British School. As the teaching staff included the vicar, the Revd F.R. Webb, MA, Mr Vernon Hicks who taught woodwork in his own workshop, and other suitably qualified persons, with Mrs Constable as attendance officer, the 'Strike' school contrived to comply with the legal definition of education. This, together with the Local Education Authority's realization that it had failed to conform with the regulations concerning the 'consultation with parents over the change of status of a school', resulted in there being no prosecutions of parents for non-attendance of their children at school. Highworth then became only the second school strike in the history of compulsory education in England.

When the buses left for Kingsdown on the first day of the Michaelmas term 1937 there were less than a score of pupils aboard whose parents were prepared for them to attend the Upper Stratton Senior School. During the next two years the number of Highworth children attending Upper Stratton increased slowly, while the 'Strike' school ran into problems of finance, premises, teachers and truancy. What the outcome would have been is very difficult to say, but the problem was overtaken by the outbreak of war in September 1939. This effectively meant that more important issues were in the forefront of people's minds, and the resulting disruption of education and life in general, together with the extra demands of children evacuated from their Stratford (East London) schools, ensured that the 'Strike' school failed to survive the war – with the exception of a small private school run as an off-shoot of the 'Strike' school by Miss Pottinger in the rear of her father's grocery shop in Swindon Street (now Mattingley and Sharps, Electricians).

The war represented years of flux for education not only in Highworth, but throughout the country. The chaos was the result of two major periods of

PARENTS with their children marching to the Highworth School yesterday.

The Highworth 'Strike' school protest march in August 1937

confusion during the early evacuations from London, the 'call-up' of local teachers, the 'blackout' and, in the early summer of 1944, the further evacuations made necessary by the threat from the V1 and V2 bombers. However, out of this chaos came the 1944 Education Act, the so-called Butler Act which promised secondary education for all, together with the raising of the school leaving age to fifteen. The 1944 Act was eventually implemented in 1947 with the vast majority of Highworth pupils receiving their secondary education at the Upper Stratton Secondary Modern School, while those who had passed the 11+ selection examination (the replacement for the so-called 'scholarship' examination) received their education at either Headlands or Commonweal Grammar Schools. A very small number who were at the secondary modern school were able by selection at 13+ to continue their education at either the Secondary Technical School, at The Lawns, Swindon, or at Adcroft Technical or Victoria Commercial School, Trowbridge, so completing the tri-partite system of secondary education envisaged by the 1944 Act.

This situation continued until the beginning of the Michaelmas term 1956, when pupils from Highworth and Blunsdon instead of transferring to Upper Stratton formed the first year of the new Highworth Warneford Secondary Modern School which was near completion in the western half of The Park. As the buildings were not yet completed the British School was once again pressed into service, until the main buildings were ready at the beginning of the Lent term when the second and third years joined them from Upper Stratton under their headmaster J. Westerby Tasker, Esq. BA.

The Highworth Warneford Secondary Modern School which opened in 1957

The Highworth Scout Troop, *c.* 1910

YOUTH ORGANIZATION IN THE TOWN

The Boy Scouts arose out of an experiment by Lieut. General Robert Baden-Powell, the hero of Mafeking, when he held an experimental camp for twenty boys – half from public schools and half from inner city areas – on Brownsea Island, Poole Harbour, Dorset in August 1907. This was followed by publication between January and August 1908 in fortnightly parts of *Scouting for Boys* based on his experience as a soldier in India and Africa. The Boy Scout Movement began impulsively, as the intention of Baden-Powell was only to provide a vehicle for existing youth organizations to use.

In Highworth the Scout Troop was founded in 1910 by Canon Stevens, the vicar of the parish church of St Michael's, and for the first thirty plus years of its existence the troop was known as the Highworth St Michael's Troop, although it was never a 'closed' church troop. The first Scoutmaster was in fact a woman, a not uncommon occurrence at that time, in this case a Miss Jebb the sister of Colonel Jebb of Westrop House, and her assistant Scoutmaster was my father Ernest Tanner.

Troop meetings were held on Wednesday evenings in the Hall at the foot of Eastrop Hill, and on Saturday mornings in the grounds of Westrop House. Their activities were typical of the Scout Movement, and included signalling, first aid, pioneering, boxing, swimming practice at the Swindon baths at 6 a.m. on Sunday mornings, with the Scouts returning for Communion at 8 a.m. in the parish church.

In 1912 the troop had a bugle band, which unfortunately was short lived, ending on a tragic note. While marching past the Freke Arms public house the band startled two dray horses which were waiting there while beer was being unloaded. Startled by the noise the horses bolted, killing the driver, resulting in the disbandment of the band.

In 1913 Lord Glenusk invited the troop to spend their summer camp at Crickhowell on the banks of the River Usk, the troop's first camp away from their immediate Highworth area. In the same year Harry Bartrop gained the troop's first King's Scout Award, his association with the Scout group lasting for some sixty years, for many of these years as Chairman, and eventually he was awarded the Medal of Merit for his services to Scouting.

In 1930 my father Ernest Tanner became group Scoutmaster, a role he carried out until his death in 1952. During this period the troop continued its meetings on Wednesday evenings, and annual camps were held in the Gower Peninsula, at Bossington on Porlock Bay, Somerset, at West Bay and Corfe Castle, Dorset, as well as short camps in the Highworth area.

For the first time ever the troop was represented at the 5th International Jamboree held at Vogelenzang, Holland by Bruce Reynolds of Hampton, and two further King's Scout Awards were gained by Ian and Vivian Trewhella respectively.

During the 1939–45 war the troop fell upon difficult times, but survived although membership dropped at one time to only four Scouts. However, throughout the whole period the troop assisted the war effort by collecting waste paper, rose hips and horse chestnuts, as well as providing 'casualties' for Civil Defence exercises.

By the end of the war the troop was in a stronger state than ever, with detached patrols in both Coleshill and South Marston. On 1 October 1946 a Senior Scout Troop was formed, which among other activities carried out a survey of local footpaths, besides producing a crop of King's Scouts – Derek Lester, John Brook, and Leslie Clark with Leslie representing the troop at the 6th World Jamboree held at Moisson in France during August 1947.

The year 1947 saw the formation of a Wolf Cub Pack with Mr Bob Harris as Cubmaster, who became group Scoutmaster in 1952 on the death of my father, and with Mrs Wendy Peaple taking over as Cubmistress, and Mr Ted Jefferies as Scoutmaster, Ted having been a member of the troop from the late 1930s until his Air Force service in 1946. Together this team led the Scout group throughout the '50s and early '60s.

THE AIR TRAINING CORPS

In 1941 the Government decided that the youth of the country should be involved either in full or part-time education, or in part-time youth service. As a means of ensuring this the Air Ministry launched the Air Training Corps as a state sponsored youth organization for air minded young men. As part of this organization the existing 210 Squadrons of the Air Defence Cadet Corps became the first 210 Squadrons of the new Air Training Corps. The newly formed squadron of the ATC in Highworth became 214 Squadron ATC hence was the fourth squadron of the newly formed ATC.

Parades were held regularly at the Council School, where classes in such subjects as the theory of flight, mechanics, meteorology, navigation, as well as drill were taught. Activities further included visits to nearby RAF stations, and when possible air experience flights, and longer camps were held at more distant RAF stations during the school summer holidays.

Sport also occupied an important place in the training of the air cadets, in particular football and boxing, and on this score Flt. Sergeant Ted Boncey reached the finals of the ATC Boxing Championships at the Albert Hall. Sadly, with the end of the war, the ATC in Highworth fell into oblivion, only to emerge from its own ashes nearly half a century later.

Can you fill in the gaps? . . . Front row, left to right: 1. unknown; 2 Bill Smith; 3 unknown; 4 Cpl John Loder or Roper; 5 unknown; 6 Flt Lt Heath; 7 FO Percy Naylor; 8 Sgt Frank Leighfield; 9 Cpl Peter Crossley; 10 unknown; 11 George Toy; 12 unknown; 13 unknown; Second row: 1 unknown; 2 unknown; 3 unknown; 4 Mr Miller?; 5 Roy Fitchett; 6 unknown; 7 unknown; 8 Mr Muir?; 9 Ted Gray; 10 Ted King; 11 Alec Midwinter; 12 unknown. 3rd row: 1. unknown, 2. Fred Jones, 3. Harold Pope, 4. unknown, 5. unknown, 6. Tony Skull, 7. Harry Gornall, 8. unknown, 9. unknown, 10. Tudor Thomas, 11. unknown, 12. Alec Chambers, 13. Les Fuller, 14. George Hilliard, 15. unknown. Back row: 1. Norman Broome, 2. unknown, 3. unknown, 4. unknown, 5. Mr Sly?, 6. Ted Gardener, 7. Frank Benford, 8. Mr Staples, 9. Mr Jordan, 10. Des Cheeseley.

214 Squadron Air Training Corps, *c.* 1943

Children's Games

From time immemorial there has been a fixed season for the traditional children's games and activities now sadly defunct.

In January hoops were in favour, while February saw the enthusiasm move to the playing of marbles in their various forms together with the collecting of buttons, which included 'sinkeys', 'shankeys', 'liveries' and 'sixers'. However with the cry 'buttons are out', March brought in whips and tops, including peg-tops, lashing-tops and humming tops, while April provided the season for a variety of skipping games. May and the lighter evenings saw rounders in favour, with June being the time for hopscotch. The summer saw children actively involved in hay-making and harvesting, although younger children would be entertaining themselves with a variety of flower games. The lessening demands of labour saw August being the time for kite flying, while the onset of autumn and the ripening of nature's bounty saw 'conkers' dominating the scene, with stories of 'hundreders', and accusations of 'baking' and 'soaking' (in vinegar).

The coming of winter saw fewer children's games, although Hallowe'en was renowned for 'ducking for apples', and December inevitably was the time for Christmas carols.

A modern fair in Highworth, c. 1950

CHAPTER FIVE

Highworth and the Railway

The coming of the 'railway age' had a profound effect on many towns and villages in the country, and in this respect Highworth was as strongly influenced as anywhere, starting in 1841 with the decision by the Great Western Railway to build its workshops at Swindon, a decision which in effect deprived Highworth of its position of relative importance in north-east Wiltshire. As a result there was recession in Highworth some 150 years before our present problems. With the Oxford to Bristol coaching trade also in steep decline Highworth was in grave danger of becoming very much a rural backwater.

As a result the nearest railway station to Highworth was that at Shrivenham, and consequently the most important road into the town became the one from Shrivenham, the present B4000 along which merchandise was brought from Shrivenham station.

In an attempt to ensure that Highworth benefited from the 'railway age' a meeting of the leading lights in the district was held in the National School on 24 September 1873. The object of the meeting was to consider the problems inherent to the building of a railway line from Swindon to Lechlade via Highworth, so joining the GWR to the East Gloucestershire Railway (the Witney to Fairford line). This project was the third involving Highworth and the railway; the two earlier suggestions in 1845 and 1864 respectively suggested a Rugby to Swindon line passing through a tunnel under Eastrop Hill and thence to the main Swindon–Paddington line, and a line from Porton on the London and South Western Railway to Fairford, with this line passing not through Highworth, but rather through Hannington.

However, as with these two earlier projects the plan for a railway through Highworth to join with the East Gloucestershire Railway foundered. It was replaced in 1875 by the formation of the Swindon and Highworth Light Railway Company, with the company's Act of Parliament for the Swindon to Highworth line receiving the Royal Assent on 21 June of that year.

Problems were soon experienced in obtaining sufficient capital to commence the building of the line, and the projected opening of the line some nine months after starting work was seen to be unrealistically optimistic. Eventually by February 1878 some £12,000 of the proposed £21,000 had been raised;

however the financial problems were not at an end, as the company needed another year before they were able to find a contractor who was prepared to carry out the necessary work, and to accept 850 shares in part payment.

Of the ceremony of 'cutting the first sod' there appears to be two accounts: Sir Daniel Gooch in his Memoirs and Diary reports that 'I went to Highworth on the 6th March to assist in cutting the first sod of the Highworth Light Railway. The day was fortunately very fine and all went off very well. The sod was cut by Mrs Hussey-Freke' (the wife of the chairman – Ambrose Hussey-Freke of Hannington Hall). However the *North Wilts Herald*'s report of the occasion is more in keeping with the eventual tradition of the line when it reports, 'A small area had been roped off for the Ceremony and near this the Directors, Shareholders, etc, had been placed in a special area with the Ladies. Such was the attendance that this place quickly became full with results which can best be described as hilarious; the ropes gave way and the Dignitaries, Ladies and others fell into an undignified heap. The band, under Bandmaster Hawkins, continued to play unconcernedly.'

A fortnight later work on the line commenced.

By 1880 the company was once again in financial difficulties, as a further £8,000 needed to be raised to pay for heavier track required by the GWR before they would work their trains over the line.

The inspection of the line by Colonel William Yolland, Royal Engineers, on behalf of the Board of Trade on 5 March 1881 caused yet further problems for the company, as he refused to pass the line as being fit for opening to passenger traffic.

As a result of this decision the company's engineer, a Mr Arthur C. Pain, left the meeting when a vote of 'no confidence' in the engineer was passed. As a consequence of his sacking Pain entered into litigation against the company, resulting in a long and acrimonious legal wrangle.

By this time the company was in very considerable financial difficulties, and somewhat reluctantly the GWR took over complete control of the line some nine months before its eventual opening on 9 May 1883.

As a result of this takeover the shareholders of the Swindon and Highworth Light Railway Company suffered a considerable financial loss, as the amount offered by the GWR represented only 24 per cent of the value of their shares.

The takeover of the line was finally confirmed by Act of Parliament in August 1882, and on 30 April of the following year the line was passed as fit for passenger traffic by Major Francis Marindin, Royal Engineers, on behalf of the Board of Trade.

The official opening ceremony for the line was arranged for Tuesday 8 May 1883 which was declared a public holiday in the town, with the line opening for public passenger service on the following day.

For the opening ceremony a special train was run, headed by two locomotives bedecked with flags and bunting and consisting of six first class saloons, four first class ordinary, and four brake coaches. The train which left Highworth at 11 a.m. carried the former directors of the Swindon and Highworth Company together with their shareholders. Enthusiasm for the long awaited opening of the railway to Highworth, some thirty-eight years after being initially mooted, was such that the bridges and embankments were crowded with well-wishers as the train passed by. The train arrived promptly at Swindon Junction station at 11.30 a.m. and returned to Highworth at 12.30 p.m.

During this time there was a procession through the streets of the town to the National School, where lunch was provided for the children as well as the men who had worked on the construction of the line. Returning to the station the train was greeted with cheers, and music from the band of the 2nd Wilts Rifle Volunteers, once again under the baton of Mr Hawkins.

At 3.45 p.m. the train left once again for Swindon this time carrying some 500 children from the area; for the majority this was their first experience of railway travel.

On their return tea and cake awaited them, at which they were joined by the local elderly folk, together with the Oddfellows and Foresters, the latter leaving on the third trip of the day at 7.10 p.m. Their return was greeted with a display of fireworks provided by the manufacturers Brook and Company.

Highworth station, *c.* 1920

Intermediate stations were opened at Stratton alongside the Ermin Street (A419), at Stanton Fitzwarren, and at Hannington, albeit the Hannington station being at Swanborough adjacent to the Freke Arms, with the village of Hannington some miles distant over the hill. Passenger trains ran some five times per day on weekdays, except that on Mondays an extra train ran from Highworth to Swindon at 9.30 a.m. for the convenience of those attending the Swindon cattle market in Old Town.

Unfortunately there was no reciprocal arrangement for the Highworth market, with the exception of 1893 when a special market train was run from Swindon to Highworth during the summer months, ceasing in October and never repeated. This lack of regular transport undoubtedly led to the demise of the Highworth market by 1926.

The first of these trains left Swindon at 7.15 a.m., and the last train arrived there at 8.15 p.m. These were all mixed trains carrying freight as well as passengers. Goods trains also ran to Highworth during the middle of the day, but these were not timetabled.

As has been described earlier many of the men from Highworth worked 'inside' – the local expression for those who were employed in the GWR Works – so that in 1890 a workman's special was introduced leaving

Hannington station

The Freke Arms, Swanborough, which was the only obvious destination from Hannington station

Highworth at 5.20 a.m. and returning from Swindon at 5.45 p.m. In the 1930s and early 1940s the streets of Highworth would be quiet at about 6.15 p.m. until the workers' special arrived, when for the next ten minutes or so the streets would echo to the sound of the steel tipped boots of the workers as they hurried home for their evening meal, when peace would once again descend upon Highworth.

In 1897 a wooden shed was built at Highworth station, large enough to hold three wagons; the shed although well used initially became redundant in the later years of the branch. The Oriental Fibre Mat and Matting Company in Brewery Street made good use of the freight trains at Highworth. The bales of coconut fibre were imported from India by way of Brentford Docks, and arrived in Swindon in a train of some twenty or thirty wagons, these being brought to Highworth a few at a time as required, with GWR lorries transferring the bales from the station to Brewery Street.

The workman's special

The Oriental Fibre Mat and Matting Company in Brewery Street

GWR lorry transporting rolls of matting to the station

The finished mats and matting were sent in covered vans to the potential buyers mainly in South Wales. So great was the reliance of the mat factory on the railway that during the General Strike of 1926 workers at the factory had to be laid off because of the shortage of raw materials. Other Highworth firms to utilize the railway were Bartrops who brought in agricultural machinery by this route, including in the 1950s two combine harvesters. The Highworth Gas Company took delivery of some 20 tons of coal per week, and the various coal merchants, Messrs Baldwin, Cook, Gilbert and Haggit, made certain that coal was carried on every freight train.

However, overshadowing all of these was the use of the railway to convey milk from the surrounding farms to London for processing. Despite the development of Marshall's Dairy in Sheep Street, the carrying of milk provided the largest single source of income for some fifty years. So large was this trade that by 1900 Sunday trains had been introduced to cope with this traffic. A further indication of the importance of agriculture to the economy of Highworth.

The workforce during a break in the weaving shed

The First World War saw the Highworth branch play its full part in the conduct of the war. Bartrops were engaged in the manufacture of horseshoes for the multitude of horses in use by the services, and an average of 24 tons per week were sent off by rail, with a maximum of some 36 tons.

At Stanton a special siding was laid to cope with the demand for timber felled in Great Wood by the Forestry Battalions; while the 'Powder Works' at Stratton provided further traffic for the Highworth branch.

The rail strike of 1919 meant that milk which had been sent to the various stations was left to go sour, and the farmers were once again affected by the 1926 General Strike, with the result that some farmers did not return to use the railway, and this seriously affected the future of the branch; and the Sunday workings introduced principally for carrying milk ceased in 1933.

In 1928 the crossing-keepers were removed from the Cricklade Road crossing, resulting in the fireman now opening the gates and the guard closing them, and the need to add time to the journey. In the same year the Bristol Tramways and Carriage Company introduced a bus service from Swindon to Highworth, which proved to be faster and more convenient than the train with resulting problems for the railway.

By the time of the Second World War the overbridges at Ermin Street and Kingsdown Road had been rebuilt, so that with the building of the Phillips and Powis factory at South Marston to produce the Miles Master III advanced trainer much of the traffic was brought to Stratton by rail, and then to the factory by road, hence effecting a vital saving of petrol. By June 1941 the factory now had its own branch line from the Kingsdown Road junction, so that materials and personnel could be brought direct to the factory.

The war saw changes in the staff on the line: for the first time young women were employed at Kingsdown Road signal box, and at Stanton and Hannington stations. Mr S.R. Toy received his appointment as stationmaster, some ten years after the retirement of Mr H.D. Mant, who had replaced Mr R. Perrett in 1904.

Sheep Street – note the cobbled footpaths, still present under the tarmac

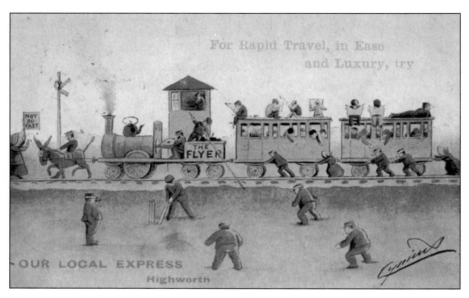

Humorous postcard celebrating the Highworth 'Bunk'

With the end of the war more changes followed: the GWR ceased to exist in 1947, road transport gained very considerable ground, and railway losses continued to increase. As a result the Western Region of British Railways announced their intention of withdrawing passenger services to Highworth, and the last public train on the Highworth line was the 6.05 p.m. on 28 February 1953.

Affectionately known to all locals as the Highworth 'Bunk' the line has produced many stories, some true, some possibly apocryphal. Such is the belief that you could dismount from the 'bunk' en route, pick a bunch of wild flowers, and still catch up the train. Probably a commentary on the delay at the Cricklade Road crossing.

Or the stories concerning how many sacks of coal were collected from the lineside in Stanton Great Wood from attempts to bring down a pheasant in the adjoining pheasant covert.

Or finally the driver 'learning the road' who missed his braking point for stopping at the Cricklade Road crossing and went through the crossing with the gates hanging on the buffer beam.

For all Highworthians of more mature years the 'Bunk' has a very special place in their memory.

CHAPTER SIX

Agriculture and Allied Trades

Basically Highworth has been throughout its history a small market town dependent upon the agriculture of its surrounding area and the trades allied to farming for its prosperity or lack of the same. Only in the years since 1940, with the increasing mechanization of farming and the change from a labour intensive industry to one which requires the input of great capital investment, has farming lost its foremost place.

Highworth standing as it does on one of the arable islands of the Upper Thames Valley, with its underlying geology of loam, stone brash and clay upon the limestone, is surrounded by the North and Mid-West Wiltshire Grass Region of the heavy clay areas.

Historical evidence of the arable farming of this island of relatively fertile loam can be found in Ogilvy's maps of the 'Salt Route' from Salisbury to Chipping Campden via Highworth, and of the 'Pack Horse Route' from Oxford to Bristol again via Highworth. These maps of 1675 and 1698 respectively show the town with arable land surrounding it except to the east, where there is pasture and common. Cobbett on his visit to Highworth in September 1826 comments that 'It is a tolerably rich . . . country' with 'some corn'. Thomas in his *General View of Agriculture of Wiltshire* (1811) describes the area as being 'the deep strong land from Calne by Broadtown to Highworth' and gives the rotation of crops on the arable land as '1. Wheat 2. Oats 3. Turnips 4. Barley 5. Clover – mown 6. Clover – fed and summer fallowed for Wheat.'

The predominance of agriculture in the area can be seen from the figures given by Thomas of persons 'agriculturally employed'. These being:

Hannington	179 men	184 women	240 agriculturally employed		
Inglesham	46 "	43 "	45	"	"
Sevenhampton	94 "	93 "	94	"	"
South Marston	116 "	136 "	150	"	"
Stanton Fitzwarren	91 "	90 "	120	"	"
Highworth	676 "	817 "	544	"	"

Rocque's map of Berkshire showing field boundaries around Highworth

Kelly's Directory of 1899 indicates that the chief crops of the farms around the town were wheat, barley and beans, together with some dairy farming, although by 1931 it was recorded as 'mainly pasture', a commentary on the decline of agriculture nationally. The outbreak of war in 1939, and the pressing need for the country to become self sufficient in foodstuffs resulted in a return to arable farming. A land utilization survey conducted by the Highworth Senior Scout Troop in 1947 clearly indicated that this imperative had occasioned the same tongue of fertile soil to be returned to arable farming as it had been before the farming decline of the post First World War period. With the Government subsidies paid to farmers in the post Second World War period this pattern of agriculture remained in force until the 'food mountains' of the 1980s and the policies of the European Economic Community enforced change on the patterns of agriculture.

Essential to the maintenance of agriculture were those trades which serviced the farmers' needs. The need for farming equipment and its repair together with the provision of ironmongery was first met in the town by the firm of Joseph Hill, who in 1910 were bought out by William La Coste Bartrop whose family firm supplied the wants of local farmers until the early 1940s, and who in the days of their shop in the High Street had supplied the

Staff of W.L. Bartrop & Co., agricultural engineers, c. 1950

requirements of the household for electrical goods, utensils, ironmongery, etc. Bartrop's also held the agency for the erection of Boulton and Paul's Dutch barns and other farming equipment such as wind pumps to supply water from local wells for the cattle in the fields. In their later days Bartrop's were at the forefront of the technological revolution which engulfed farming, and the supply and repair of tractors, combine harvesters, grain driers, etc. became their stock in trade.

Before the tractor became dominant the horse held sway in farming, and the provision of saddlery and harness was the province of the Woodbridge family in their shop in the High Street. The family business continued until relatively recent times doing shoe and leather repairs as work horses reduced in number, before succumbing to changing times and becoming a newsagent's shop.

The essential shoeing of the working horses was carried out in the blacksmith's shop in Brewery Street immediately behind The Fox public house; as the use of horses decreased the forge was only used on a part-time basis, and now has become part of the public house. Evidence of another forge is provided by Forge Cottage in the Elms, which has an attached outbuilding which was originally used as a forge, although not in living memory. However the outside of the outbuilding still has the iron ring to which the halter was attached, with the blacksmith carrying out his work in the open air.

Mr E. Woodbridge at work in his saddler's shop in the High Street

At work in the blacksmith's forge

Opposite The Fox and the blacksmith's forge, in an area now occupied by the Threshold Carpet Factors offices, was Hill's wheelwrights yard. The wheelwrights selected and seasoned their own wood, ash and oak for the framework of the body of the wagon, elm for the flooring and the heavy, transverse part of the undercarriage, with ash for those parts taking the knocks and strains, such as the rails and ladders, and for the pole which joins front and back of the wagon. The same three woods were used for the wheels: elm for the naves, oak for the spokes and ash for the felloes.

The sawyers worked 'top and bottom', sawing laboriously hour after hour down the length of a felled trunk which was secured in position over a saw-pit, producing planks of equal and even thickness. Seasoning was a long process, as it was usual to allow one year for every inch of thickness. The apparent chaos of a wheelwright's yard was a most unlikely setting for the superb craftsmanship of the wheelwright. The wheelwright's skill and reputation was centred on his ability to make a wheel and to so perfectly construct the axle-beds that when the wheels were 'hung' the whole carriage ran as it should. The wheel was tyred with an iron hoop, put on hot so that as the tyre cooled and contracted the felloes and spokes were forced home tighter than could ever be accomplished with a sledge hammer.

Hill's wheelwrights yard at the junction of Brewery Street and Shrivenham Road

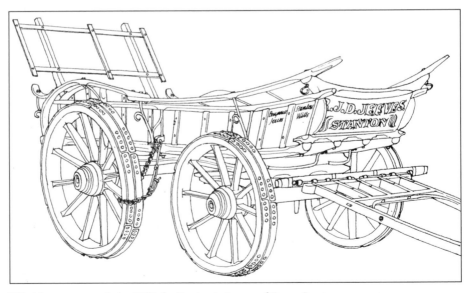

Wiltshire wagon made by Hill's for Benjamin Jeeves of Farm, Stanton

The entire wagon was so constructed that any component part, wood or iron, could be extracted for replacement or repair. No part was ever secured by the use of glue. As with everything else about their lives, the wagons they made changed but slowly, and with knowledge passed on from father to son everything was instinctively made to last. When everything was finished the painter contributed his share to give its gay proud coat of paint. The Wiltshire wagons made in the Highworth yards had a blue body, with red underframe, wheels and ladders, and the farmer's name and farm lettered in either white on black, or in yellow.

Highworth had two wheelwright's yards up to the outbreak of war, the other being that of Joe Woolford in Cherry Orchard where the workshop was a thatched building near to the Glebe Field. As the demand for horse-drawn agricultural vehicles declined, wheelwrights became general carpenters making gates, wooden household articles and coffins, with the wheelwright taking on the role of undertaker as well.

Rope manufacture was also an essential requirement of agricultural life. Philip Frankis was a rope manufacturer with a rope walk alongside Lechlade Road; the building was about forty yards long, a very simple building, little more than a long narrow shed, with a tarred felt roof. Here the craft of rope making had been carried on since 1800, and probably earlier. The rope making technique differed little from that employed in the old-time rope walks. At one end was the wheel, plus simple appliances to help the spinners in their work, which produced ropes for general farm work, horse reins, wagon lines, hay nets, calf slips (used on calves when they are sent to market) and halters of all sorts. So the best traditions of an old and honourable craft are preserved.

Philip Frankis was not however the only rope manufacturer in the town, Harry 'Scruggy' Rouse, whose shop was the last on the southern side of the High Street, sold a similar list of wares to those made by Philip Frankis.

For many years an essential adjustment to the farming way of life was the 'hiring fair'. Highworth fairs were held on 13 August for cattle, and on 11 October for cattle and hiring of servants, and a market was held every fourth Wednesday. The Highworth 'hiring fair' is described by Alfred Williams·

. . . All the men and boys who went to be hired wore whip-cord in the coats or hats; by this the farmers knew they were in search of a situation, and accosted them, and engaged them on the spot. I only went to the fair once to be hired and then I was unsuccessful, as it was past noon when I got there, and all the hiring was over by midday; if you were later than this hour, you stood precious little chance of obtaining a situation. When the

Lechlade Hill with Frankis's rope walk on the right hand side

farmer wanted a man – these used to stand in a line along the edge of the pathway displaying their badges of whip-cord – he walked down the street, eyeing them all up and down till he saw one that pleased him; then he went up to him and asked him a series of questions – where he had worked, and for how long, whether he was married, the number and age of his children, and what he expected to receive in wages; if the other accepted it the bargain was considered as made: there was no setting the bond aside afterwards.

The Highworth market in recent times had a chequered history, for despite the efforts of the Market Committee the market struggled in the face of competition from Swindon. The relative remoteness of Highworth from the main GWR line caused problems for the market in the 1850s and '60s, and it was felt than an extension of the railway to Highworth would be instrumental in saving the market. However, the coming of the railway to Highworth in 1883 showed no evidence that it had stimulated the market.

In March 1893 the monthly cattle market was again revived, but trade represented only one tenth of that of the 1859 revival. However the market settled down well, amounting to some 50 cattle, 100 sheep, 100 calves and 40 head of poultry, and continued in this small way until well into this century, with the Christmas Market being the highlight of each year.

The wild flowers of the area are typically those of the meadowland and fringe of the chalk downs. However, during the Second World War the

Spectators making their way to the VWH Hunt (Cricklade) point to point

ploughing of pasture land for the growing of crops led to the loss of the early purple orchis from the fields around Fresden, and of the Snake's Head Fritillary from fields close to the River Thames at Inglesham. More recently the common cowslip has been lost from the Sevenhampton fields as a result of aerial crop spraying. Unimproved hay meadows are now also rare in the area, and in particular that clear indicator of the hay meadow – quaking grass-brisa media. Sadly the last three of these unimproved hay meadows in Botany Fields have been sacrificed in the development of a local authority golf course.

Fox hunting, traditionally a sport of the countryside, has flourished in the Highworth district with the Vale of White Horse Hunt, Cricklade, which until recently met at the Market Place, the Freke Arms, Fresden and Sevenhampton, the latter being the only local meet still in being. Further the VWH Hunt staged its point to point at Burytown Farm in 1923 when HRH the Prince of Wales (later King Edward VIII) rode in the members light weight race, and finished second. Immediately before the Second World War in 1937 and 1938 the VWH Hunt held its point to point meeting at Queenlaines Farm. However, the war-time drive for more arable land meant that with the return of peace there was no return of steeplechasing to Highworth.

In 1871 the Duke of Beaufort's Hunt ran their quarry to ground near Highworth in a run of some 14 miles from Grittenham Great Wood via Brinkworth Common, Somerford Common, Bradon Lodge and Cricklade. The run was recognized as one of the outstanding runs of the nineteenth century.

CHAPTER SEVEN

The Architecture of Highworth and District

For a general appreciation of Highworth and its buildings one cannot do better than read again John Betjeman's description of the town when he writes:

> I have never seen Highworth given due praise in guide books for what it is – one of the most charming and unassuming country towns in the West of England. It is unspoiled. The only ugly things are too many electric light and telegraph wires zig-zagging across its High Street.
>
> Highworth is extraordinary because it has more beautiful buildings than it has ugly ones.
>
> Highworth is full of old inns with big bay windows. It would not surprise me to see periwigged men in knee breeches and ladies in silks and countrymen in smocks walking about.
>
> Even the Matting Factory is tucked away out of sight. So is the church.
>
> Highworth is the CENTRE of some of the loveliest country around its feet – Coleshill House in Berkshire, Great Coxwell barn, the oldest and grandest tithe barn in Britain . . . Inglesham church down by the Thames, the church which William Morris saved from so-called restoration. Countless unknown lanes lead up the hill to Highworth.
>
> When I am abroad and want to recall a typically English town, I think of Highworth. Ah, Highworth as a whole! Churches and chapels, doctors' houses, Vicarage, walled gardens with pears and plums, railway station, inns and distant cemetery, old shops and winding streets.

I listened to Betjeman's original Sunday evening broadcast in 1950, incidentally missing evensong to do so, and very little has changed in the intervening years.

Gone fortunately are the electric light and telegraph wires zig-zagging the High Street, as is the railway station, an early casualty of Beeching's re-organization. Gone as well is the mellow light of the old gas lamps which so suited the old town, to be replaced by the very lamp posts which Betjeman so hated. Gone also are the immemorial elms, those wonderful avenues of Hangman's Elms and Friar's Hill, casualties of the scourge of Dutch Elm disease. There has been one benefit as a result of the opening up of new vistas – in particular the views of the Wiltshire and Berkshire Downs together with White Horse Hill which in days gone were hidden from view by the ubiquitous elm. Most sad of all is the loss to fire of Coleshill House only a brief two years after John Betjeman's eulogy. In essence, however, little has changed, the visitor from a 'time capsule' would still recognize the quintessential Highworth!

After this eloquent overview of the buildings of Highworth and district, now to some of its individual attractions.

St Michael's and All Angels Parish Church – This handsome fifteenth-century church is on the site of an earlier twelfth-century Norman cruciform church, the extent of which was very roughly that of the present chancel. All that remains of this building is an original window opening on the left of the altar, and twelfth-century tympanum with Saxon art work of a man gripping a lion by its jaws under an arch of twining flowers, which is thought to represent Samson and the lion, although Arthur Mee believed it to be David fighting the lion. The tympanum is now placed over the south door to the church. As with most churches of this period building was spread over a considerable number of years. The south porch is from the fourteenth century, above which is the priests room complete with a piscina with a drain from it (where the priests washed the sacred vessels), a fireplace, and a 'squint' which enabled the priest to view the interior of the church. The main body of the church is fifteenth century, when probably between 1440 and 1480 the church was

Norman tympanum, presently above the south door of St Michael's

extensively rebuilt, including the building of the west tower in Perpendicular style with a fan vault inside probably replacing an earlier crossing tower. Fragments of the parapet of the original south aisle can be seen on the outside staircase leading to the belfry.

There are three recesses in the walls of the church, where most probably the church plate was stored for safety. Two are at the east end, and one in the side wall to the vestry. The church plate consists of a silver-gilt pre-Reformation chalice of 1523 with a crucifixion and Man of Sorrows engraved on the foot, a sixteenth-century plain paten and a seventeenth-century flagon together with a communion cup and two salvers.

In the chancel are three misericords representing a mermaid, an angel, and a bearded head, and a Norman buttress is outside the south-west of the church.

The church register at Highworth dates from 1539, and is said to be the best kept and oldest dated register in England. Such registers of baptisms, marriages and deaths were first ordered to be kept by Henry VIII in 1538.

Music to rival Nebuchadnezzar's orchestra might at one time have been heard in the church. There, more or less harmoniously, sounded forth the violin, key-bugle, clarionette, bassoon, bass-violin and a trumpet known as 'The Serpent'. Armed with these strange instruments the choir occupied one of the two galleries, while the parson occupied the other. Two of these instruments were still in the possession of Mr William Boulton the grocer in the late 1920s. The church has a peal of eight bells, with the following inscriptions: fourth bell: 'This bell recast 1898. Francis Charles Master, Vicar, Robert R. Elwell, James J. Powell, Churchwardens'; sixth bell: 'John Bagley made mee 1689. Come when I call, make no delay; To serve God all kneel down and pray.' Tenor bell: 'To the Glory of God and memory of Revd John Sloper, of Westhay, Berks, 1798–1877, this bell was recast by his son, G.O. Sloper 1898.'

The south transept window has figures of King Alfred, Richard Coeur de Lion, and St Michael in memory of the three sons of James Brown JP of Eastrop Grange who lost their lives on the Western Front in the First World War.

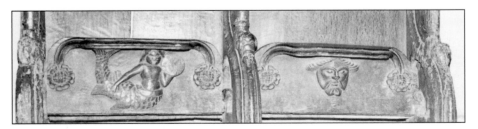

Misericords representing a mermaid (left) and a bearded head (right)

The east window, a gift in the 1930s of the Misses Hambridge of Queenlaines Farm, depicts St Michael vanquishing the dragon, surrounded by the risen Christ, with panels depicting the professions, motherhood, the care of the sick, and the artisans, and with the coats of arms of the Bishoprics of Gloucester, Salisbury and Bristol. Also a gift of the Misses Hambridge is the rood screen carved by a local butcher Vernon Hicks of Westrop.

★ ★ ★

Two of Highworth's oldest houses are those at the east end of the High Street running down to Eastrop, and dated 1652 and 1656 respectively, on one of which is the sign of the 'Leather-seller's Boy'. When Mr Tovey was living in one of these houses he found two coins in the ceiling and plaster of the wall. One room of the house has bottle-glass panes in the windows, and a very fine fireplace. There are also mullioned and transomed windows, and diagonal chimney-stacks. Although having the appearance and datestone of a mid-seventeenth-century house, it is in fact a fifteenth-century hall house with two floors inserted in the east end in the seventeenth century. In the nineteenth century the house was divided into four, but returned to one house in 1969. Here in 1666 was a butcher's shop, from which the first meat was sent to London after the Great Fire. From this Highworth earned its Charity to the value of £300 per year, held by Trustees.

Facing the other end of High Street in the southern end of Lechlade Road is the Jesmond House Hotel, originally Higgs the tailors, an early eighteenth-century town house with four bays, two brick storeys, and a large doorway with fluted Doric pilasters, frieze and pediment. Further to the north in Lechlade Road is another four-bay brick house – the White House – and after that the early eighteenth-century Highworth House, appreciably taller, with five bays, three storeys high with quoins and segment headed windows, a panelled parapet and a plain doorway. Over the years this house has been the vicarage, a garage, a private school and a private house. A little further north used to be Home Farm, a charming three-bay stone house with brick trim, with a porch on very thin Corinthian posts. Sadly this was demolished to make way for the Home Farm housing development.

At the west end of High Street is the Zion Congregational chapel (now the United Reform church), built of stone in 1825, with arched windows and a pedimented gable. Next to the Zion chapel is the Highworth DIY shop, which outside at least remains the same as when it was Willis's, an archetypal nineteenth-century grocery shop. This is followed by what Pevsner claims to be 'the finest house in Highworth', Inigo House, for many years the doctor's surgery. Similar in design to Highworth House but appreciably more ambitious. Of early eighteenth-century construction it is four bays wide and

Home Farm, now sadly demolished to
make way for recent housing
development

three storeys high with segment headed windows with aprons. The doorway
has Corinthian pilasters and a broken-back segmental pediment, a big top-
cornice and a panelled parapet. Internally there is an excellent staircase with a
wrought iron railing.

The next building of interest is the King and Queen Inn, a coaching inn
with clear evidence of coaching use. Long and irregular, with a two-storey
canted bay, plus another projecting bay with the porch beneath it, the King
and Queen is almost certainly fifteenth century as a plank-and-muntin
partition alongside a cross passage confirms the earlier date.

Facing the market place is the Saracen's Head, another inn from the
coaching period, with once again clear evidence of its use, brick faced of two
storeys and with a central archway.

A short way into Westrop on the eastern side is Chantry Cottage, which
can conceivably lay documentary claim to being the oldest dwelling in the
town. The chantry of William Ingram was founded in 1453, and the cottage
became part of a parcel of land purchased by Thomas Reve and George
Cotton after the dissolution of the monasteries. Westrop Farmhouse some
short distance north is an early seventeenth-century building which is said to
date from 1640, with stone mullions, drip moulds and relieving arches; very

possibly it may have been an earlier building as there is evidence of a cross passage.

In Cricklade Road we find Westrop House, an early nineteenth-century stone building of six bays and two storeys, with a semi-circular porch raised on plain Doric columns. The back of the house which adjoins Cricklade Road has two canted two-storey bay windows. Built by William Crowdy in 1818, William Cobbet was a guest at Westrop House in 1826 when conducting his 'Rural Rides'.

Westhill House – Built in 1790 as the Highworth Workhouse, and designed in the Cotswold style, it has a Cotswold stone tiled roof with dormers, and the walls are rendered stone rubble with long and short quoins and brick chimney stacks.

The workhouse was built as a result of an 1789 Act of Parliament, and the only house in the town having this distinction cost the parish £1,900 to build. It continued in the role of the parish workhouse until 1835 when,

Chantry Cottage, Westrop, possibly the oldest dwelling in the town

Westrop House

The Vicarage, Highworth.

Westhill House

under the new Poor Law, Swindon and Highworth were joined in the Poor Law Union. As Westhill House was the only suitable property it continued in use for the larger union, becoming in the process very overcrowded with as many as eighty inmates at any one time.

By 1847 the Highworth Workhouse was too small for the needs of the growing town of Swindon, and a new and larger workhouse was built at Stratton St Margaret.

By 1880 Westhill House was in use as the Highworth Vicarage, later to become the home of the Arkell family after Redlands Court, and eventually the home of the late Sir T. Noel Arkell.

Close to Westrop House is another of Highworth's older vernacular buildings in the shape of Elm Cottage. Dating from 1645 the cottage was at one time used as a forge, the present sitting room bearing the evidence of this period. During the 1940s the cottage was owned by the composer Colin Campbell, brother of Admiral Campbell RN famed for the use of 'Q' ships during the Great War. Elm Cottage boasts a fine wisteria, and may well have been alluded to by John Betjeman in his broadcast on Highworth!

Hannington Hall – Built in 1653 by the brothers Raufe and William Freke. The east front is still in its original state with the exception of the entrance, which however may have been in the central canted bay of the symmetrical front. Interestingly, although it was built during the period of the Commonwealth, it contrasts with Coleshill House which was built at approximately the same time in the Palladian style by Roger Pratt.

Hannington Hall

The south side originally possessed neither the bays nor the porch, nor the balustrade and inscription. The inscription, which reads, 'Henry Freke C.B. built this wing in memory of his ancestors', was added by Colonel Henry in 1836 together with the coat of arms of his wife's family, the Smeatons. In 1863 a further wing consisting mainly of servants' quarters was added, as was the fashion at the time, only for part of this wing to be demolished some one hundred years later by the present owner.

Hannington Hall was used to billet the ATS radio operators who were to maintain contact with the Auxiliary Units in the event of 'Operation Sealion' becoming a reality.

St John the Baptist, Hannington – This was designed by Slater and Carpenter in 1869–71, using many of the original parts, for example, the late Norman south doorway, with the traditional zigzags at right angles, which meet and form broken lozenges. It has an early thirteenth-century Norman doorway with a round arch but with Early English mouldings, and a priest's doorway all of the thirteenth century with a pointed arch. The west tower has an open spiral staircase designed by Slater and Carpenter.

Coleshill House – Described as one of the most splendid of seventeenth-century houses, it was the work of an amateur Sir Roger Pratt, who had spent the years of the Civil War in France, Italy and the Low Countries. Returning about 1650 he began Coleshill House for a relative and although he consulted Inigo Jones in the process the house was undoubtedly Pratt's work. Two major innovations were included: the old great hall was transformed into a staircase hall, with a very Italian feeling, and a fine double sweep of the stairs climbed round the walls to a first floor landing. Behind the hall was the Great Parlour, the two separated by an inter-connecting corridor. Pratt himself called this type of design 'a double pile' or 'double cube', the dimensions being 124 ft long and 62 ft wide and of four storeys. The main lines of Coleshill House were horizontal, not vertical, with no mock battlements, Gothic or Tudor arches, or other architectural devices. Sadly Coleshill House was destroyed by fire on Wednesday 24 September 1952, the fire resulting from a workman's blow lamp melting the lead on the roof while he was in the process of carrying out repairs to the house. Unfortunately the supply of water to fight the fire was insufficient, and as a result Coleshill House was lost to the National Trust and the locality.

St John the Baptist Church, Inglesham – This has stood for over seven hundred years at some distance from the village of Inglesham. The Norman nave has box pews and a small Jacobean pulpit complete with a canopy. The aisles,

The grand staircase at Coleshill House

each with its canopied piscina, are enclosed by fifteenth-century screens with a design of carved flowers. The thirteenth-century chancel has tall and slender altar rails, box stalls with carved tops, and a canopied piscina. The font is medieval, but the cover dates from the sixteenth century.

There are traces of patterns on the wall, and a sculptured relief showing the Madonna with the Hand of God reaching down to bless the child, and a sundial etched into one corner. This together with its weatherbeaten appearance indicates that the relief had spent much of its time outside.

Warneford Place – The original family home of the Warneford family, all that presently remains is the so-called ballroom which is early eighteenth century. It was the right wing of a house of nine bays with a pedimented three-bay centre, and there was a left wing as well with five bays of brick and stone, with arched windows. The stables date from 1734, although the shaped gables are not of that date.

Fresden Farmhouse – This is an Elizabethan farmhouse with a flat symmetrical front with a gabled porch and mullioned windows. There is also an Elizabethan dovecote with a lantern.

Bibliography

Betjeman, J., *First and Last Loves*, Murray, 1969.

Gibson, *Warneford, VC*, Fleet Air Arm Museum, 1979.

Haslam, J., *Wiltshire Towns*, WANHS, 1976.

History of Highworth, vols 1, 2 and 3, Highworth Historical Society, 1981.

Hopkins, H.R., *Highworth*, Vorda Press, 1926.

Lampe, *The Last Ditch*, Cassell, 1968.

Mackay, *The History of the Wiltshire Home Guard*, Wiltshire T.A., 1946.

Pevsner, N., *The Buildings of England – Wiltshire*, Penguin Books, 1975.

Smith and Heathcliffe, *The Highworth Branch*, Wild Swan Publications, 1979.

Williams, A., *A Wiltshire Village*, Duckworth, 1912.

Willis's grocers shop, High Street, Highworth